GALAPAGOS

the enchanted isles

David Horwell

Dryad Press Limited   London

The Islands series

What have these people in common: Enid Blyton, Daniel Defoe, Robert Louis Stevenson and Roy Plomley? They have all written about islands, islands as places of adventure or fantasy. Think for a moment of the many stories or events that are associated with islands. What do you know about "Fortress Falklands", or Alcatraz, or the adventures of Robinson Crusoe? Islands have long held a special appeal and this series sets out to explore the fascination of islands.

Every island is unique, with a different location, a distinctive history and a particular personality. And yet about them all there are similarities, too. Island cultures are distinct because they are isolated, set apart from mainstream societies. They can be remote, places of refuge or sanctuary, where you can "get away from it all"! Monks and rich recluses have chosen island homes because they wanted seclusion. Other island inhabitants have had no choice in the matter because the isolation of islands also makes them ideal places for imprisonment or exile; Alcatraz and Elba certainly have that one thing in common.

In many cases, too, the remoteness of islands has meant that life for people, animals and plants has remained undisturbed by the progress and change of the mainlands. Forms and ways of life survive which elsewhere have become extinct, as is the case on the remote and beautiful islands of the Galapagos.

Another common feature of island life is that it can present similar problems of survival. Is there enough land to grow food and to keep animals? Is there an ample supply of water?

Why do islands become deserted?

Islands, therefore, can be places of challenge where you must learn to survive, fending for yourself on limited resources, or places of isolation and retreat where you dream about the good life — and listen to your desert island discs!

In each book of the series the author's purpose is to explore the uniqueness of a particular island and to convey the special appeal of the island. There is no common approach but in every case the island can be seen as a system in which a society is linked to its physical environment. An island culture can show clearly how the natural environment influences the ways people make a living. It also shows how people learn to modify or change that environment to make life better or more secure. This is very much a geographical view of islands, but the ideas and study skills used in the books are not limited to those of the geographer. The one controlling idea of the series is that islands are special places; small enough to know well and varied enough to illustrate the rich diversity of environments and lifestyles from all parts of the world. Islands can be places of social experiment or strategic importance, of simple survival or extravagance. Islands are the world in miniature.

John Bentley
Series editor

For details of other books in the Islands series, please write to Dryad Press Limited, 8 Cavendish Square, London W1M 0AJ.

Contents

ACKNOWLEDGMENTS

This book would not have been completed without the help of my mother, Doreen Horwell, and the encouragement of my wife Iolanda.

I would like to thank Roger Jameson for sending me out to Galapagos in the first place, and Julian Fitter who gave me a job on his yachts. Special thanks to Mr Corley Smith, of the Charles Darwin Foundation, for his suggestions on chapters 5, 6 and 10. Thanks too, to David White for sharing his knowledge, the late David Kiehn for his jazz out there, and Fausto for his Pizzeria.

This book is dedicated to all Naturalist Guides in Galapagos, past and present, and the hope that the islands will be protected for ever.

All photographs on the cover and inside the book are by the author, with the following exceptions: Figures 28 and 30 are courtesy of Down House; Figure 31 is from A.E. Brehm's *Merveilles de la Nature* (1885); Figures 33 and 39 are from Darwin's *Zoology of the Voyage of HMS Beagle* (1840); Figure 34 is by Roger Perry (courtesy of the Charles Darwin Foundation). The blue-footed booby in the Frontispiece is by Hilary Brandt, and Figure 46 was inspired by the drawings of Peter Scott.

Cover photographs

The photographs on the front cover show: the view from Bartolomé; sea lion mother and cub; blue-footed booby and tourist. The photographs on the back cover show: male frigatebird with display pouch; and tortoise and keeper at the Charles Darwin Research Station.

British Library Cataloguing in Publication Data

Horwell, David
    Galapagos : the enchanted isles.
    1. Galapagos Islands, to 1987
    I. Title

    ISBN 0-85219-771-3

Typeset by Tek-Art Ltd, Kent
and printed and bound in Great Britain by Richard Clay Ltd, Chichester, Sussex
for the publishers Dryad Press Limited,
8 Cavendish Square, London W1M 0AJ

ISBN 0 8521 9771 3

1

Islands at the middle of the world

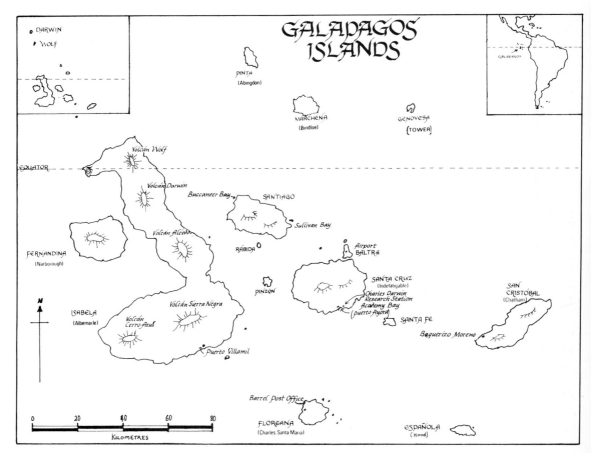

1   *The Galapagos archipelago.*

One thousand kilometres out into the eastern Pacific lies a remote group of rocky islands. They are the tips of huge undersea volcanoes, some still smoking with a sulphurous steam, as at the very beginning of the Earth. For most of their history they have been inhabited only by strange reptiles, bright red crabs and thousands of birds. These islands were called "enchanted" because of their strange mists and treacherous currents, then later were named after their giant inhabitants; "Galapagos" is Spanish for tortoise.

Their inaccessible position and lack of fresh water kept man way from the islands until he found he could exploit some of the animals there — tortoises, seals and whales. The Galapagos became a sanctuary for pirates and hunters, and were also used as a penal colony. These are themes we shall examine later.

The islands are special because of their geographical setting. This was realized by the naturalist Charles Darwin on his visit in 1835. He, more than anyone, is responsible for the islands' fame, as they helped to inspire his theory on "The Origin of Species", later known as evolution.

Today this bizarre volcanic landscape is visited by tourists from all over the world, who come to see the fearless wildlife and experience a part of the Earth that is an unspoilt natural wilderness.

Location

The Galapagos Islands are an archipelago, that is, a group of several islands. Look them up in your atlas (either on the page showing the Pacific Ocean, or on the page for South America). Which is the country nearest to them? They lie 1000 km west of the continent of South America, off the coast of a small republic called Ecuador, to which they belong. This country is named after the Spanish for "Equator", the line which passes through both the country and the islands. Look at the map of the Galapagos archipelago, Fig. 1, and find which island lies right on the Equator.

On maps the islands are officially named as *Archipelago de Colon* (that is, "Columbus Archipelago" in Spanish), in honour of the discoverer of America — although he never went anywhere near them. But everyone still uses the popular name, Galapagos.

The Equator is an imaginary circle on the Earth's surface, and lies midway between the North and South Poles. It divides the Earth into northern and southern hemispheres. For purposes of navigation the Equator is taken as zero degrees latitude.

Lines of latitude are imaginary parallel lines around the Earth. In nautical terms, latitude is measured as the angle between the Equator, the centre of the Earth and the place being measured (see Fig. 2). Latitude is given in degrees, and the North Pole is at 90°N. What latitude is the South Pole?

Lines of longitude, or meridians, run north to south through both poles and are all the same length. They are measured as an angle from the meridian at Greenwich in London, which was agreed to be 0° longitude during the early days of sail.

The Galapagos archipelago is situated at 0° latitude, and is approximately 90°W.

Size

As we are dealing with an archipelago, rather than a single island, we are considering an area of ocean at least 200 km across. The islands vary in size considerably. The largest is called Isabela, and is J-shaped; it is really five big volcanoes that have joined together. The longest part of Isabela measures 134 km, and the widest part 42 km. This island has a larger area than all the others combined, 4,588 sq. km. The total area of land in the archipelago is 7,882 sq. km.

There are four other large islands, each (except San Cristobal) composed of a single volcano and roughly circular in outline. The biggest of these is Santa Cruz, 32 km in diameter and 986 sq. km in area. San Cristobal is one of the oldest islands and has been eroded into a more irregular shape. What are the other large islands called? See Fig. 1. There are a further 12 islands that range in size from 1 sq. km to 173 sq. km. That makes a total of 17 islands, but there are other islets and rocks which are too numerous to mention. The highest part is on Isabela. It is the summit of Volcan Wolf at 1,707 m above sea level.

Appearance

"Take five-and-twenty heaps of cinders dumped here and there in an outside city lot;

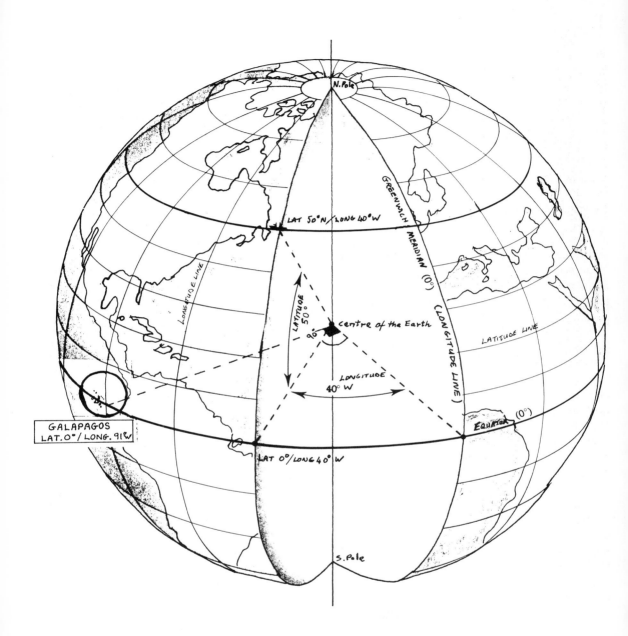

Labels within the diagram:

N.Pole

LAT 50°N / LONG 40°W

GREENWICH MERIDIAN (0°) (LONGITUDE LINE)

LONGITUDE E. LINE

LATITUDE 50°

90°

centre of the Earth

LONGITUDE 40° W

LATITUDE LINE

EQUATOR (0°)

GALAPAGOS LAT. 0° / LONG. 91°W

LAT 0° / LONG 40° W

S. Pole

imagine some of them magnified into mountains, and the vacant lot the sea; and you will have a fit idea of the general aspect of the *Encantadas*, or Enchanted Isles. A group rather of extinct volcanoes than of isles, looking much as the world at large might, after a penal conflagration"
(Herman Melville, 1841)

2 A cut-open diagram of the Earth, showing how angles of latitude and longitude are calculated.

Clearly that old sea-dog did not think much of the islands. To the early visitors, expecting to find a tropical paradise, they were a disappointment. "A shore fit for

Pandemonium," was Captain FitzRoy's comment in 1835 when he came with the more enthusiastic Darwin on the *Beagle*. But even Darwin admitted, ". . . Nothing could be less inviting than the first appearance". He was aware of their volcanic origin, though: "I scarcely hesitate to affirm, that there must be in the whole archipelago at least two thousand craters. . .".

The reason these visitors were so disparaging about the islands was that they saw only the desert-like lowlands, where there is no moisture and hardly anything grows. As you go up to the higher parts of the larger islands the atmosphere becomes more humid. The vegetation changes from cactus and thorny scrub to a mixture of bushes and trees and, at the highest parts, grassland, ferns and mosses. All Melville saw was ". . . tangled thickets of wiry bushes, springing up among deep fissures of calcined rock, and

3   Tagus Cove on Isabela island shows the unspoilt beauty that has attracted visitors from afar.

treacherously masking them; or a parched growth of distorted cactus trees".

The younger and more volcanically active islands, such as Fernandina, have not had time to develop much plant cover. Fernandina has one of the most active volcanoes in the world. A lot of it is undisturbed volcanic lava and ash. When I climbed up to the crater I saw footprints of other scientists from previous years that had been "fossilized" by volcanic debris.

Despite the islands' having repelled people for so long, their unspoilt, rugged beauty and tame wildlife attract modern visitors, the tourists. They fly out from Ecuador, which takes under three hours, and enter a world which gives the impression that they have landed on another planet. Few are disappointed that they made the journey.

2

The Galapagos setting

Not only is the Equator an imaginary line which is useful to navigators; it is also a meeting place for vast wind and ocean systems of the northern and southern hemispheres. Galapagos lies just south of this convergence.

The sun heats the equatorial regions (low latitudes) more than the polar regions (high latitudes) because of the curved surface of the Earth. The reason for this can be seen in Fig. 4. At the Equator a ray of sunshine hits a smaller area of the Earth than a similar ray does at a point further north or south. In other words, as one goes towards the polar latitudes the sun's rays are spread over a larger area.

The Earth, which is hottest at the equatorial regions, heats the air above it. Because warm air is lighter than cool air, it rises and is replaced at sea level by cooler, heavier air. This constant movement of cool air towards the Equator forms the Trade Wind belt. Find out why these winds were called the "Trade Winds".

Global wind patterns

Look at Fig. 5, which shows the pattern of the Earth's major winds. As you can see, the Trade Winds do not blow straight towards the Equator, but hit it at an angle. This is because the Earth's rotation deflects the winds to the right of their path in the northern hemisphere and to the left in the southern hemisphere. This deflection is called the "Coriolis effect", after the French mathematician who first studied it. A similar effect can be experienced on the centre of a moving roundabout; if you try to walk towards the edge you will find yourself moving sideways as you move outwards.

Because these winds blow from the east, they are also known as "north easterlies" and "south easterlies".

Where the two Trade Wind belts meet, the winds are light and variable. It was here, in this

4 Why the sun seems hotter at the Equator. Measure the width of the two beams of solar energy. Measure the length along the Earth's surface (the shaded area) of where each beam hits the earth. Is there a difference between the low latitude beam and the high latitude beam?

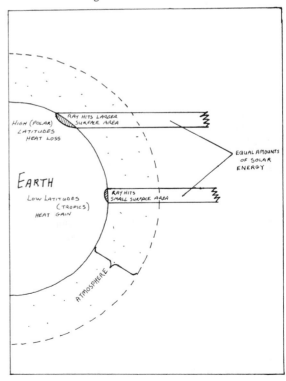

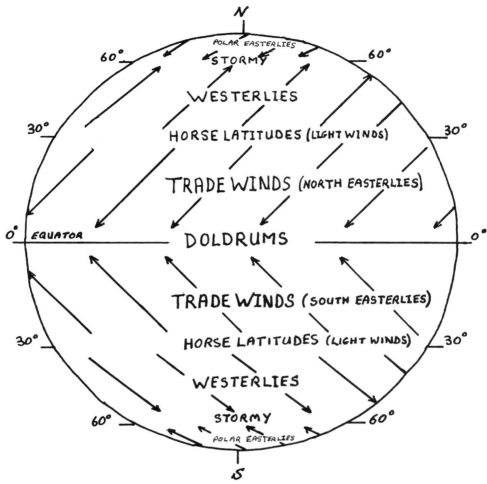

5 The Earth's major winds at sea level. Find out why the "Horse Latitudes" are so named. In which parts of the world are winds strongest and therefore most dangerous to sailors? Where does Britain appear in the wind patterns? How does this affect our climate?

area called the *Doldrums*, that sailing ships used to be becalmed. The Doldrums coincide roughly with the Equator, but in the region of Galapagos, they lie further north for most of the year.

Ocean currents

Ocean currents are caused by the surface waters of the oceans being dragged along by the prevailing winds; the currents become deflected even further, because the water is also·subjected to the Coriolis effect. The wind-driven currents, deflected by Coriolis, are then blocked by land masses and so turn into a gigantic circular motion called a "gyre". Look at Fig. 6. Which currents make up the South Pacific Gyre? If you were to throw a message in a bottle into the sea from Galapagos, where might it be found?

The Peru Current and upwelling

The Peru Current flows up along the west coast of South America. Its general course can be seen in Fig. 6, and the way it affects Galapagos can be seen in Fig. 7. Oceanographers have divided it into a coastal and an oceanic current, depending on the distance from land. The Peru

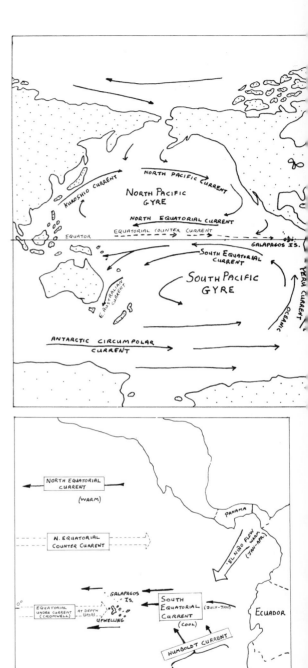

6 The Pacific Ocean, showing the main currents. ▶
How does Australia affect the South Pacific gyre?
Why would it be difficult to sail from Galapagos to
Tierra del Fuego in South America?

Current is one of the world's greatest currents.
It is also known as the Humboldt Current, after
the famous German explorer Alexander von
Humboldt, who first realized its importance.

As the Trade Winds drive the current
northwards, the Earth's rotation tends to pull
the waters to the west, away from the coast.
Cold water from the deep comes up behind to
fill in the space. This *upwelled* water, as it is
known, is full of nutrients, and as we shall see
in chapter 8, this promotes the growth of a rich
marine life. The fisheries of Peru are some of
the most productive in the world.

This cold but fertile water reaches
Galapagos, now as part of the South Equatorial
Current (see Figs 6 and 7), and turns otherwise
desert islands into a paradise for marine and
coastal wildlife.

The Cromwell Current

In Fig. 7 we can see a current that hits
Galapagos head-on from the west, but only at
depth. Find it. Although it is technically known
as the *Equatorial Undercurrent*, it is usually
called the *Cromwell Current* (after the
oceanographer who discovered it in 1952).

Though it is a relatively narrow stream of
water, it is very important to Galapagos as it
brings deep, nutrient-rich, cool, upwelled
waters to the west of the archipelago. The
current replaces waters moved to the west by
the South Equatorial Current. It is not as
constant as the other currents, but it is so
significant that the Galapagos cormorant and
penguin breed only when it arrives. These
animals have a way of knowing when the
Cromwell Current is coming, something we
cannot yet do.

7 The main currents that affect Galapagos. ▶

Climate

These ocean currents are largely responsible for the climate of the Galapagos, which are not typical wet tropical islands. Many are true desert islands, too dry to support much plant life. Only the larger islands, which have a lot of cloud cover, are able to develop trees.

Fig. 8 shows graphs of rainfall and temperature. We can see that there are two distinct seasons: a hot rainy season from January to April and a cooler, dry season from May to December.

Look at Fig. 8 and answer the following questions: Which is the wettest month? Which month has the highest average air temperature, and how hot does it get? In which month does the sea surface temperature get warmer than the average air temperature? Do you notice anything else about that month?

The cool "garua" season

From May to December the air and sea are coolest and at this time there is often a mist called *garua* present. It hardly ever rains, however.

The Trade Winds are constantly blowing and keep the cool waters of the Peru Current heading towards the Galapagos. The air in contact with the ocean is cooled, with the result that warm, sub-tropical air is overlying cool air, a situation known as a temperature

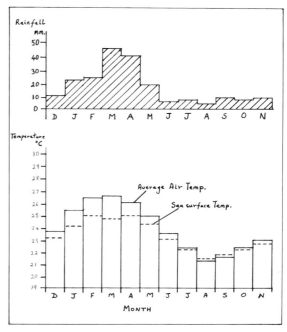

8   Climate graphs for Galapagos. Why do you think there is a difference between the temperature of the air and sea surfaces?

9   The relationship between winds, cold currents and moisture, or garua, and their effect on the vegetation of the islands. Can you explain why the vegetation zones are higher on the north-west side of Santa Cruz?

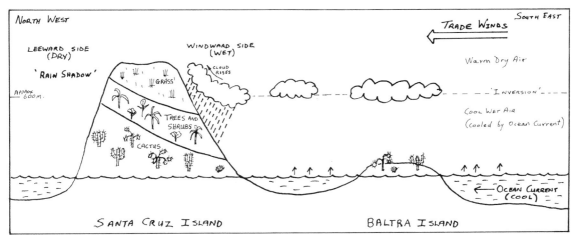

inversion. At the junction where cool air meets warm air, moisture collects and forms stratus clouds at about 300-600 m above sea-level.

When the clouds are blown towards land, such as on the larger islands, they are forced to rise and form drizzly mist or *garua*. This is why only the taller islands, such as Santa Cruz, get enough moisture to support permanent vegetation. Can you see why the larger islands should be wetter and have more vegetation on the south-east sides?

The north-west sides are drier and said to be in the "rain-shadow", as by the time the air-stream gets there it has shed its moisture. On a larger scale the whole of Fernandina island is dry because it lies in the rain shadow of Isabela.

10   *Clouds forming over Isabela at the inversion layer.*

The hot season

From January to April is the warm season. The south-east Trade Winds are less strong, and, therefore, so are the currents driven by them. Warmer water comes down from the Panama Basin, which lies to the north-east. Sea temperatures rise to 25°C and the air temperature to 30°C. The inversion layer is broken up and the skies become blue and clear, with some cumulus clouds and occasional rain showers. With the seasonal movement of the sun the Doldrums shift south to include Galapagos and bring the convection rain of the tropics. Convection rain occurs in hot climates, when moisture evaporates in the heat of the day and falls as rain in the afternoon as the air cools. This is an almost vertical circulation of water.

Once the rains have come to Galapagos the islands become transformed; plants which look dead, such as the "Palo Santo" tree, suddenly sprout leaves and flowers appear.

El Niño

A warm current which comes at around Christmas time is known as *El Niño*, which means "the Christchild". It comes every year, but once every six or seven years is an "El Niño Year", when the flow is exceptionally large. Temperatures and rainfall soar, which is good for life on land, but catastrophic for life that depends on the sea, as all the fish move away. Seabirds, marine iguanas and sea-lions cannot raise their young, and many die. The effects are even more serious in Peru, where the fishing industry collapses. 1982/3 was one of the most damaging El Niño years.

Scientists from the research station in Galapagos (see chapter 10) are constantly monitoring all life on the islands. They were particularly interested in the effects that the 1982/3 El Niño had on wildlife there. They report that things are only now getting back to normal.

We have seen how atmosphere, ocean currents and weather are all related. Galapagos, with its mixture of warm and cool currents and upwelled waters, has a unique setting. This determines what wildlife is able to survive there. Also, as we shall see in Chapter 9, the number of species of wildlife which were able to reach the islands in the first place were limited by the islands' remoteness.

3

Volcanic origins

The ocean floor

If we could pull out a gigantic "plug" in the Pacific and drain the ocean, we would find an impressive variety of scenery: mountains taller than Everest, valleys deeper than the Grand Canyon and ridges longer than the Alps. This underwater landscape tells us a lot about how the Earth's surface is made. In this chapter we will see how this surface, or crust, is not a permanent structure but is being constantly created in deep-sea volcanoes and elsewhere

11   *Bathymetric chart of the Galapagos Islands.*

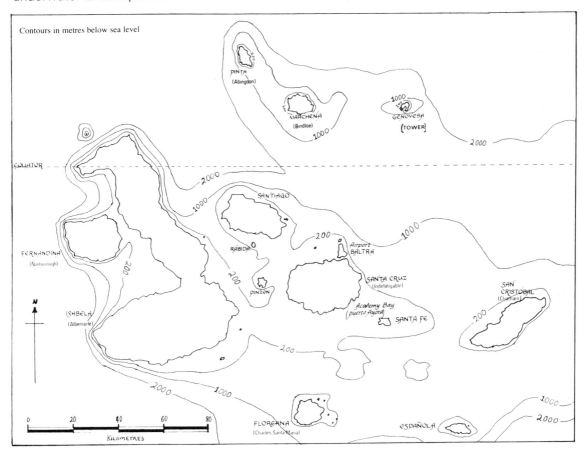

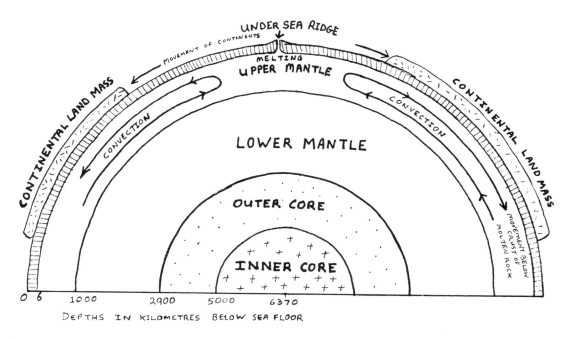

UNDER SEA RIDGE

MOVEMENT OF CONTINENTS

MELTING
UPPER MANTLE

CONTINENTAL LAND MASS

CONTINENTAL LAND MASS

CONVECTION

CONVECTION

CONVECTION

LOWER MANTLE

OUTER CORE

INNER CORE

MOVEMENT BELOW CRUST OF MOLTEN ROCK

0 6   1000   2900   5000   6370

DEPTHS IN KILOMETRES BELOW SEA FLOOR

destroyed or "swallowed" back into the bowels of the Earth. We shall also see how it was responsible for the formation of the Galapagos.

The Galapagos are the tips of gigantic undersea volcanoes. In earlier times a platform of volcanic rock was built up, about 200-400 m

12   A simplified section of inside the Earth.

below sea-level. On top of this platform individual volcanoes grew and eventually broke

13   Section through the Earth's crustal plate in the Galapagos region.

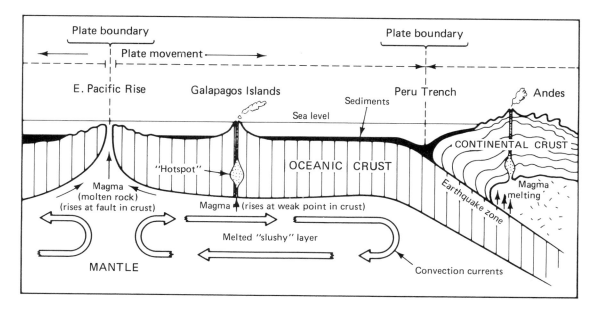

Plate boundary

Plate boundary

Plate movement

E. Pacific Rise

Galapagos Islands

Sediments

Sea level

Peru Trench

Andes

CONTINENTAL CRUST

"Hotspot"

OCEANIC CRUST

Magma (molten rock) (rises at fault in crust)

Magma ↑ (rises at weak point in crust)

Earthquake zone

Magma melting

Melted "slushy" layer

MANTLE

Convection currents

above the water, some now reaching heights of 1600 m above sea-level. Look at Fig. 1, where the major volcanoes are marked. Which island is made of five volcanoes that have joined together?

For sailors it is very important to know the depths of the sea-bed, especially in strange waters, and so underwater relief maps are made. These are known as *bathymetric charts*. A bathymetric chart for waters around Galapagos is shown in Fig. 11. The curved lines represent depths below sea-level, just as contours represent heights above sea-level on a regular map.

Look at the chart, Fig. 11. Which islands are included within the same continuous 200 m contour? (This is called the "Galapagos Platform".) Is the sea deeper between Fernandina and Isabela islands or between Isabela and Pinta islands? To the south-west the undersea platform dips steeply to great depths, greater than 3000 m, whilst to the north-east it dips more gradually.

The Earth's moving surface

To us, living on the apparently hard crust of the Earth, the ground beneath us seems fairly solid stuff. In fact, below this hard outer crust is a layer of warmer, "slushy" rock, melted by the heat of the Earth's interior. This can be seen in the layer called the "upper mantle".

The outer crust may be hard, but it is cracked or split into gigantic sections called "plates". These plates are irregular in shape. There are about six major ones, and numerous small ones. It is at the edges of these plates, where they either split or collide, that earthquakes and volcanoes occur. The crust is thinnest under the oceans and thickest where continents are found. The land masses, largely composed of granite, ride like "rafts" on the denser rock of the oceanic crust.

All these plates move, ever so slowly (between 2 cm and 10 cm per year), pushed around by the enormous forces in the hot layers below. New crustal material is pushed

up into gaps formed where the plates crack open. This happens along undersea ridges such as the East Pacific Rise, near Galapagos (see Figs 13 and 14). Other cracks occur where pieces of a "plate" slide past each other without molten rock appearing. These are called "faults".

If new crust is being pushed up along the ridges of the sea floor, then it follows that old crust must disappear elsewhere, to prevent it all buckling up. This "crust-swallowing" occurs at the bottom of the sea, where it can be found along trenches at the edges of continents, such as the Peru Trench off South America.

As oceanic crust is pushed underneath the continental land mass, the friction causes both earthquakes and heat which melts some of the overlying crust so that it eventually rises to form volcanoes, this time on land. (See, for example, the Andes Range in Fig. 13.)

Deep-sea trenches illustrated in Fig 13 are found all around the Pacific Ocean. They go down to depths as great as 11 km below sea-level.

14 *How plate movement causes a "hotspot" to form a line of volcanoes.*

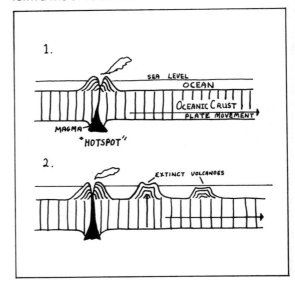

The Galapagos "hotspot"

Where does Galapagos fit into the "plate theory"? The Galapagos archipelago is situated near the boundary of three major "plates" (the Pacific to the west, Cocos to the north and Nazca to the south-east). The islands are not part of the undersea ridges, but are a separate "hotspot". As the crust moves over the hotspot, the heated rock melts and is pushed out as a volcano.

Scientists still have to discover what makes the crustal plates move and why hotspots occur where they do.

Volcanoes

The hot, molten rock that comes up from the Earth's interior is called *magma*. When it reaches the surface, the drop in pressure causes a lot of gases to be given off, rather like opening a bottle of fizzy drink. In Galapagos the magmas give off their gases easily and produce a lava that flows well. Lava is the name given to magma that reaches the surface. In areas where gases are retained in the lava, the eruptions tend to be more explosive. Most of Galapagos is made of gentle, sloping lavas that

have cooled into a black rock called *basalt*. There are sometimes small-scale explosive eruptions on the side of the main volcano.

Galapagos is one of the world's most active volcanic regions. The following is a description written in 1825 by Captain Benjamin Morrell. He was on his way to the South Pacific, and nearly met a sticky end while observing an eruption on Fernandina island (then known as Narborough).

"Our ears were suddenly assailed by a sound that could be equalled by ten thousand thunders bursting upon the air at once; while, at the same instant, the whole hemisphere was lighted up with a horrid glare that might have appalled the stoutest heart! I soon ascertained that one of the volcanoes of Narborough Island, which had quietly slept for the last ten years, had suddenly broken forth with accumulated vengeance.

The sublimity, the majesty, the terrific grandeur of this scene baffle description. . .

My men stood gazing, speechless and bewildered with astonishment and dismay. The heavens appeared to be in a blaze of fire, intermingled with millions of falling stars and meteors; while the flames shot upwards from the peak of Narborough to the height of at least two thousand feet in the air. . .

15 A typical Galapagos volcano.

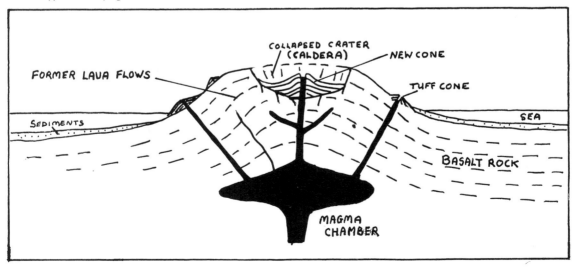

16   Sullivan Bay, Santiago island. A field of "pahoehoe" lava, cooled into fantastic shapes. This flow is about 100 years old.

17   James Bay, showing tuffstone formations eroded by the sea.

The boiling contents of the tremendous cauldron had swollen to the brim and poured over the edge of the crater in a cataract of liquid fire. A river of melted lava was now seen rushing down the side of the mountain, pursuing a course to the sea. . . The ocean boiled and roared and bellowed. . .

The *Tartar's* anchorage was about ten miles to the northward of the mountain, and the heat was so great that melted pitch was running from the vessel's seams, the tar dripping from the rigging. . .

Our situation was becoming more critical and alarming. Not a breath of air was stirring to fill a sail. . . The mercury continued to rise, the air increased to 123 degrees. Our respiration became difficult. . .

At length a light breath was announced . . .

the canvas began to feel the air and the *Tartar* began to move . . . for which we felt grateful to Heaven."

What do you think would have been the fate of the men had a breeze not arrived?

The oldest eruption we can date was on James Bay on Santiago island. The explorer Thor Heyerdahl found fragments of marmalade pots within the lava. These had been stashed away by buccaneers in 1684, and so the eruption must have occurred some time after that date. (This must be the only case where marmalade pots have been used to date a rock!) Another documented eruption was from Volcan Wolf in 1797.

The islands have also been active more recently. In 1968 Fernandina was again the scene of action, this time witnessed by scientists. They saw the volcano blow its top off and enlarge its crater by nearly two cubic kilometres! A total of 53 eruptions have been

18   The crater of Fernandina. Fernandina is one of the most active volcanoes in the world. The black area on the left is a recent lava flow.

sighted since the early 1800s, but many more must have happened unheard, judging by the number of craters. Some islands, like Bartolomé, look more like the surface of the moon.

Lava features, cinder and ash

As lava flows, its surface cools and stops flowing, but below that it remains molten and continues to flow. The surface gets wrinkled like the skin of custard in a saucepan. These wrinkles harden with the lava, giving fantastic shapes like coiled ropes, to marvel at as we walk over them. Geologists have borrowed the Hawaiian term *pahoehoe* (pronounced *pa-hoy-hoy*), for this ropy texture. (See Fig. 16.) Galapagos provides fine examples of this.

Another kind of lava flow is not pleasant to walk over; it is extremely rough and jagged and will cut you to ribbons should you fall. This is called *aa* (*ah-ah*). It is rough because the lava is sticky, a property known as viscosity, and therefore cools without flowing very far. Viscosity depends on the chemical composition and amount of gases in the lava.

"Spatter-cones" are small explosive eruptions, like pimples on the side of the main volcano, and are composed of a viscous material called cinder. (See Fig. 50.)

Explosions may also throw out fine particles, called ash, which fall down in showers like hailstorms. The ash collects in layers, blown by the wind into a cone around the vent. This hardens into a rock known as *tuff*. Some islands, like Daphne Major, are made of one big tuff cone. Despite its name, tuff is much softer than lava and is more easily worn away. (See Fig. 17.)

Uplift and subsidence

In 1954 a film crew was sailing along the west coast of Isabela when the members noted a curiously white stretch of shoreline. They investigated and found that the whole beach had been raised out of the sea and lifted by 4 m. The white colour was caused by corals and shells left stranded. Fish were found flapping in the rapidly drying pools of water. Such a phenomenon is not unusual in volcanic regions, where the surface responds to movements of magma deep below.

On the highlands of Santa Cruz island there are examples of where the opposite has occurred — large circular depressions called "pit-craters" have sunk hundreds of metres. These occur where the weight of solid rocks makes them collapse into the space left by an empty magma chamber below.

Erosion

All rocks are worn away by the forces of nature such as wind, waves and rain. The final products of erosion in Galapagos can be seen on the beaches, in the many coloured sands. The strangest are made of black sand, eroded from basalt; bright red sands come from cinder and yellow from ash (tuff), whilst pure white sands are derived from coral and shells. If I collected three samples of sand from Galapagos beaches, one red, one white and one black, which of them do you think is non-volcanic in origin?

The lack of moisture on the lowlands means that there is little erosion and hence no soil builds up. We find instead cacti and bare lava.

The highlands of the big islands, as we saw in chapter 2, do receive moisture and rain. Here there is physical and chemical breakdown of the rocks, and enough soil is produced to support dense vegetation. Geology, the climate and life are all inter-related.

4

Discovery: early visitors, pirates and hunters

Indians

The first people to set foot on the Galapagos Islands were probably South American Indians from the coastal desert of northern Peru. They were excellent sailors, using balsa rafts. We know they visited these and other islands, as fragments of their pottery have been found. They were probably on fishing expeditions and did not stay. Their conquerors, the Incas, may also have paid the archipelago a visit; a legend, passed down by word of mouth, tells of one of the Inca Kings, Tupac Yupanqui, going on an expedition to "Islands of Fire". But there is some doubt as to whether the islands he got to were really Galapagos. Knowing about the setting of Galapagos, which would have been easier for a raft equipped with just one sail and a few oars: to get out to the Galapagos or to return?

The Spanish

We have a written record that the islands were discovered accidentally by Tomas de Berlanga, the Bishop of Panama, in 1535. He was on his way to Peru when his ship was becalmed and swept 500 miles off course by the currents. His letter to the King of Spain was far from enthusiastic about the islands:

"I do not think that there is a place where one might sow a bushel of corn, because most of it is full of very big stones and the earth there is much like dross, worthless,

because it has not the power of raising a little grass but only some thistles."

In spite of this initially depressing picture, he goes on to describe the giant tortoises, iguanas and the tameness of the birds.

Like most of the early arrivals, Bishop Tomas and his crew arrived thirsty and disappointed at the dryness of the place. Two crew members died of thirst, and on the return journey there was only wine to drink. He did not give the place a name. The islands first appear on a map in 1574, as "Islands of Galapagos", but the Bishop's report was soon forgotten in Spain, where they had more urgent matters and reports of other new lands laden with gold to fill their imaginations.

Just over a decade later a group of renegade Spanish, escaping the wrath of their

19 The Galapagos hawk, one of the creatures that impressed the early Spanish visitors to the islands.

commander, drifted to the islands. They were led by Diego de Rivadeneira, who also wrote about the "smoking islands" and was struck by the beauty of the hawks. These visitors were able to quench their thirsts with tortoise blood and cactus fruits.

The buccaneers

"Twas gold was the bait that tempted a pack of us Merry Boys, near three hundred in number, being all soldiers of fortune."

Thus Captain Sharp summed up the motive of the buccaneers in 1680. These were gentlemen pirates, who would, with the unofficial blessing of the English King, attack Spanish treasure ships and relieve their arch-enemies of some of their gold (which had earlier been stolen from the Incas). They used the Galapagos as a hide-out. Why would the Galapagos have been a good place for them to seek refuge or use as a base for attacks?

Some of the pirates wrote literary accounts

20 *Buccaneers' Cove on Santiago island. This bay was used by pirates when repairing their ships.*

of their voyages. One such was William Dampier. He sailed with Ambrose Cowley and other infamous persons on the aptly-named *Bachelors' Delight* in 1684. They anchored north of James Bay in what is still known as Buccaneers' Cove. Although no gold has been found there, smashed drinking vessels and storage jars have been dug up as evidence of their carousing. It was a good spot as there was plenty of firewood, a safe anchorage and a supply of fresh water.

Dampier also found the wildlife worth writing about:

"We found multitudes of guanoes [iguanas] and a land turtle or tortoise. . . . I do believe there is no place in the world that is so plentifully stored with these animals. The guanoes here are fat and large as any that I ever saw; they are so tame that a man may knock down twenty in an hour's time with a club. The land turtle are here so numerous that 500 or 600 men might subsist on them alone for several months. . . . One of these creatures will weigh up to two hundredweight. . ."

Clearly at that time there were no thoughts about conservation. As far as the islands' ecology is concerned, the worst thing the pirates did was accidentally to let ashore black rats, who found the tortoise and iguana eggs easy prey.

When Dampier returned to England he had little to show for his years of piracy, except his writings. He published them and thus found more fame and fortune than he ever had outside the law.

Naming of the islands

Each of the islands has had several names, both Spanish and English, in the course of its history. This can cause a lot of confusion when one looks at old maps. Cowley and the "Merry Boys" of the *Bachelors' Delight* were the first to visit many of the islands, and they named them after English Kings and aristocracy or

Island names and their origins

English name	Origin	Spanish name	Origin
Albemarle	Duke of Albemarle	Isabela	Queen Isabela of Castille
Barrington	Admiral Barrington	Santa Fe	The pact of Santa Fe
Charles	King Charles II	Santa Maria or Floreana	
Chatham	William Pitt, first Earl of Chatham	San Cristobal	Patron of sailors, or after Christopher Columbus
Cowley	Ambrose Cowley		
Daphne	HMS *Daphne*		
Duncan	Admiral Duncan	Pinzon	Pinzon Brothers
Hood	Admiral Hood	Española	Spain (España)
Indefatigable	HMS *Indefatigable*	Santa Cruz	Holy Cross
James	King James II	Santiago or San Salvador	The first island discovered in America
Jervis	Admiral Jervis	Rabida	Convent of "Rabida"
Narborough	Admiral Narborough	Fernandina	Fernando de Aragon (King of Spain)
Tower		Genovesa	Genoa, birthplace of Columbus

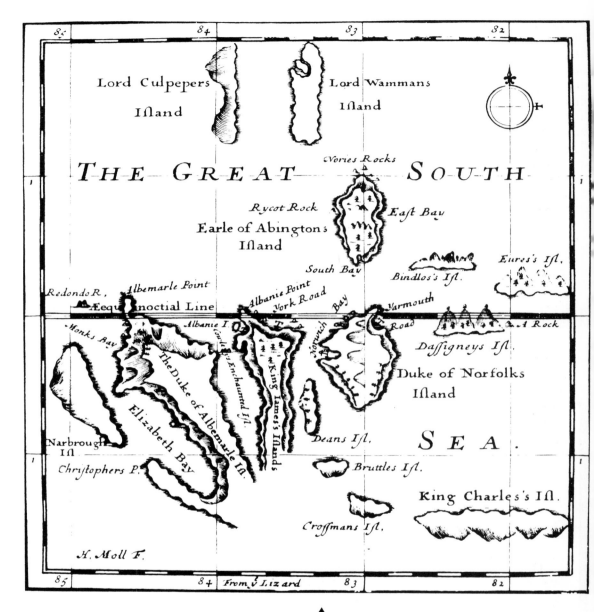

The map shows:

THE GREAT SOUTH

Lord Culpepers Island

Lord Wammans Island

Vories Rocks

Rycot Rock

Earle of Abingtons Island

East Bay

South Bay

Eures's Isl.

Bindlos's Isl.

Redondo R,

Albemarle Point

Æquinoctial Line

Albanie Point

York Road

Yarmouth Road

Monks Bay

Albanie I.

Cowleys Enchaunted Isl.

Norwich Bay

A Rock

Dassigneys Isl.

The Duke of Albemarle Isl.

King Iames's Islands

Duke of Norfolks Island

SEA.

Narbrough Isl

Elizabeth Bay

Deans Isl.

Chrystophers P.

Bruttles Isl.

King Charles's Isl.

Croffmans Isl.

H. Moll F.

From ye Lizard

famous captains of the day. Cowley explains:

"Thereupon we stood away to the Westward, to try if we could find those Islands the Spaniards call Gallapagos or Enchanted Islands, when after three weeks' sail we saw land, consisting of many islands, and I being the first to anchor there did give them all distinct Names. . ."

21 Cowley's chart of the Galapagos islands. Compare this with a modern map (Fig. 1) and see which islands are most accurately drawn. Some of the English names are different from those in the box on page 23, as islands were often renamed. The Equator is called the Equinoctial Line here. Find out the difference.

The reason the Spanish called the islands "Enchanted", meaning "bewitched", is that for much of the year they are surrounded by mists and so it seems that islands appear and disappear as if by magic. Also, the tides and currents were so confusing that they thought the islands were floating, and not "real" islands. Cowley produced a navigation chart which was the first map of the archipelago.

The name of the island group has also undergone changes. When Ecuador claimed them in 1832, they were known as the "Archipelago del Ecuador", but in 1892 were renamed "Archipelago de Colon" (the Spanish for Columbus), in honour of the anniversary of the discovery of the Americas (though Columbus never came near these islands). But "Galapagos Islands" has remained in common use.

Whalers and hunters

"I frequently observed the whales leave these islands and go Westward and in a few days, return with augmented numbers. I have also seen whales coming, as it were, from the main . . . as if they were in haste to reach the Galipagoes."
(James Colnett)

In 1793 the English Captain, James Colnett, was sent by the Royal Navy to the Galapagos to investigate their whaling possibilities for the merchants of the City of London. Though he was sent for commercial reasons, he found time to make a report on scientific matters and make a more accurate navigation chart. He began a period of exploitation that was to last until about 1870. The whalers and, later on, sealers, were to do irreparable damage to the islands' wildlife.

Whales were attracted by the plankton-rich upwelling currents. The Galapagos became a favourite haunt of the sperm whalers, one of whom was Herman Melville, the creator of *Moby Dick*.

As well as whales, the tortoises were an obvious attraction to sailors in the days before refrigeration or canned food. Tortoises could be

22 *The Post Office Barrel on Floreana island is adorned with carved names of yachts that have passed by. For nearly 200 years visiting boats have passed on mail. (The original barrel has been replaced.)*

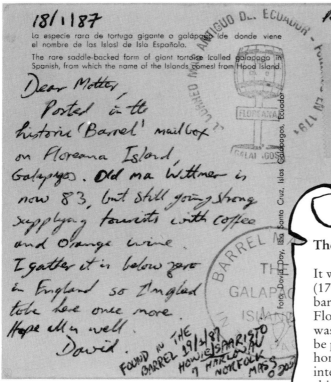

The handwritten postcard reads:

18/1/87

La especie rara de tortuga gigante o galápago (de donde viene el nombre de las Islas) de Isla Española.

The rare saddle-backed form of giant tortoise (called galapago in Spanish, from which the name of the Islands comes) from Hood Island.

Foster: Please put name & date below ▼

Dear Mother,
    Posted in the historic 'Barrel' mailbox on Floreana Island, Galapagos. Old ma Wittmer is now 83, but still going strong supplying tourists with coffee and orange wine. I gather it is below zero in England so I'm glad to be here once more. Hope all is well.
    David.

FOUND IN THE BARREL 19/4/87 HOWIE & ARISTO 7 MARLOW AU NORFOLK MASS

Foto: David Day, Isla Santa Cruz, Islas Galapagos, Ecuador

23   Postcard posted in the Barrel mailbox.

kept alive on board ship for periods of over a year, even without food or water, and so were a source of fresh meat. As more English, and then American, vessels arrived, hundreds of thousands of the creatures were removed. First one race (sub-species), then another, became extinct, and several others were brought close to extermination by man's thoughtless greed. Those which were not eaten were melted down to make cooking oil.

Equally ruthless, the fur seal hunters continued the slaughter and brought the seals dangerously close to extinction. In 1825 one captain boasted of killing 5000 seals in two months! At this time it was thought that God had created other animals purely to serve man's purposes and needs and, like the pirates, the hunters had no thoughts about the harmful effects of what they were doing.

The introduction of goats, pigs and cattle to

The Post Office Barrel

It was during the visit of Captain Colnett (1793) that a curious post-box made of a barrel was put up on a tree stump on Floreana (Charles). The purpose of this was to enable letters left by passing ships to be picked up by other ships returning home. The Americans used it to gain intelligence about the English whaling ships they were attacking in 1813.

Today there is a replacement barrel in "Post Office Bay". It has been decorated by visiting yachts, and the custom of mail delivery is carried on. Imagine you have been at sea for six months, and arrived in the Galapagos. Write a postcard to a friend back home telling him of your impressions.

some islands, with the idea of providing more meat for the future, was almost as destructive. These domesticated animals went wild and rapidly stripped the vegetation on which the reptiles fed. At this time no one owned the archipelago, and even after Ecuador had claimed the islands in 1832 there were no laws governing them. It was not until more than a hundred years later that laws were made to protect the animals (see chapter 10).

5
Refuge: castaways and convicts

From books such as *Robinson Crusoe*, we all have romantic notions of what it would be like to be a castaway on a desert island. In reality, being left on an island far from the comforts of civilization can have its drawbacks. Lack of food, water and the company of others can make people sick, lonely and even mad. Several people marooned together can either work as a team, or drive each other crazy. The assortment of people who made Galapagos their home, either by accident or by design, showed that the stress arising from the harsh environment caused disputes and violence.

Imagine that you are a castaway on a desert island. How would you cope? List the first things you would do on arrival. Make a list of ten things you think you would like to take with you to improve your life there. If you were going to a remote island, would you prefer to be alone or with others?

Patrick Watkins

The first permanent resident in Galapagos was marooned on Floreana island in 1807. He was an Irishman called Patrick Watkins. Left on his own he turned to drink for solace. We learn about this odd character from the journal of Captain Porter, who was on the American ship *Essex* chasing the British whalers (the USA was at war with Britain in 1812). Porter tells us how Patrick Watkins built himself a crude hut and grew vegetables which he swapped for rum or cash with passing ships.

"The appearance of this man, was the most dreadful that can be imagined; ragged clothes, scarce sufficient to cover his nakedness, and covered with vermin; his red hair and beard matted, his skin much burnt from constant exposure to the sun, and so wild and savage . . . that he struck everyone with horror. . . . He seemed to have no desire beyond that of getting drunk."

Watkins captured men who came ashore by offering them his potent brew until they had drunk enough to make them pass out. Then he hid them until their ships could wait no longer, In this way he acquired four "slaves" whom he put to work for him. Later he stole a boat and set sail with his captives. When this boat landed at Guayaquil, on the mainland, he was the only one on board. Whether he murdered his crew as drinking-water ran low, or ate them to survive, we will never know! He is known to have taken up with a "tawny damsel" in Peru, but was eventually put in jail there.

Convicts and colonists

Because of their isolation, islands make good prisons. How would you prepare to escape from an island? In 1832 a retired General decided to start a colony in Galapagos, and this became Ecuador's first claim to the isles. His name was José Villamil. He took out a band of condemned men and political prisoners to act as labourers. The islands then became a dumping-ground for undesirables. To survive, the colonists grew fruits and vegetables, as Watkins had, but this was not easy because of the frequent droughts. Name another island that has been used as a prison.

When the young Charles Darwin arrived in 1835, during his epic voyage around the world, there were between 200 and 300 inhabitants.

"It appears that the people are far from contented . . . the houses are simple, built of poles and thatched with grass . . . part of their time is employed hunting the wild pigs and goats which abound. . ."

General Villamil left his colony under the charge of a man called José Williams. For his own protection from the convicts he had a pack of dogs, so that it became known as the "Dog Kingdom". He was a cruel overseer, intent only on his own gain. At this time the tortoises became extinct on Floreana and some of the settlers went to other islands in search of food. Those who remained revolted against the tyrant and he fled. When the General returned, the colony had broken up.

Some settlers made a success of living on Chatham (San Cristobal) island. It was here that another dictator, Manuel Cobos, took charge in 1869. He too got his come-uppance for his brutal treatment of workers he had flogged to death: the others murdered him. Do you think the colony would have succeeded better if the labourers had not been convicts?

A more peaceful era began after the turn of the century. A new settlement was started on the largest island, Isabela and these settlers became farmers and fishermen. There are people living there still. They grow coffee, sugar, cocoa and fruits, and also raise cattle, many of which have reverted to the wild. Domesticated animals which revert to the wild are known as *feral*. In chapter 10 we shall see how a conflict of interests arises between farmers and conservationists.

Back to nature

In 1924 the book *Galapagos World's End* was published. The author, William Beebe, gave a colourful account of the islands and their wildlife. Spurred on by this, many city-dwellers dreamed of setting up a new life there, more in tune with nature, although few would achieve it.

A group of immigrants arrived from Norway – they were optimistic in thinking that stories of barren, waterless lava had been exaggerated – and were determined to make the venture work. They had schemes for developing the archipelago with fish-canning factories and farms. Unfortunately, when they arrived and saw the rocky, cactus-covered terrain, they realized it was not going to be an easy life. Many died of starvation and thirst, many returned home, and only three survived. Though the Galapagos possess a wild beauty and are a paradise for zoologists, for those who choose to stay there life is hard.

24 Papaya, one of the tropical fruits grown on the islands since the days of Villamil's colony.

25 *This lone cactus on barren lava shows the difficult terrain the early colonists faced.*

Murder and mystery

Of all the historical figures who lived on the islands, none are stranger than the Germans who came to Floreana during the 1930s. The first of three groups was an eccentric philosopher called Dr Ritter and his girlfriend Dore. Ritter was a vegetarian and nudist who, to avoid any dental problems, pulled out all his teeth and replaced them with a steel set!

Next came a family called the Wittmers, who had a sickly son named Harry. They thought the climate would do him good. Frau Margret Wittmer gave birth in Galapagos to a son called Rolf. Dr Ritter refused to help deliver the baby, and soon relations between the two families soured.

Strangest of all was the next arrival, the Baroness Eloise Wagner-Bousquet. Claiming to be an aristocrat, she arrived with two men. She proclaimed herself "Queen of Galapagos", which did not go down well with the other two families. She would take all the gifts left behind by rich American visitors, who used to call by in their yachts. The Ritters and the Wittmers became jealous of her, and the Baroness's lovers, Phillipson and Lorenz, fell out with each other.

One day in 1934 the Baroness and Phillipson disappeared. The other man, Lorenz, was left in a state of shock and became anxious to leave. A Norwegian offered to take him away in his boat, but that was never seen again, and later two dried-up bodies were found on the distant island of Marchena. If Lorenz had been responsible for murdering the others, his secret went with him.

Dr Ritter evidently knew something, and called for an inquiry, but he, too, died, in an ironic twist of fate. Having given up his vegetarianism, he ate some chicken and promptly died of food poisoning. His friend Dore returned to Germany and wrote a book about these events, but did not really explain what happened.

The role of Frau Wittmer's family in these goings-on is also a mystery. What is certain is that she and her children are all who have survived until today. She now runs a guest-house for tourists.

The war and after

In 1941 the Japanese attacked Pearl Harbor, and the United States became directly involved in the Second World War. The rest of the Americas was now under threat. The Panama Canal was the lifeline of trade for all the Pacific states, and the Galapagos made a good base for its protection. For this reason, Ecuador allowed the USA to build an airbase on Baltra (S. Seymour) island. Unfortunately, a lot of the animals were used for target practice by bored servicemen, and so today there is little wildlife on Baltra. The airstrip is still in use by the Ecuadorians and foreign tourists, who are now

27　Modern houses and outboard motors have brought change to these European colonists who have lived on Santa Cruz for over 40 years. They still prefer to scull across Academy Bay, however.

26　The airstrip on Baltra island, north of Santa Cruz. It was built by the Americans during the Second World War, and today is just big enough for the jets that bring in tourists each day.

concerned with protecting the wildlife.

Today about 6000 people live in the archipelago: about 2500 on Santa Cruz, the rest on three other large islands, San Cristobal, Floreana and Isabela. Most of these are Ecuadorians who have arrived during the last 25 years to work in fishing and tourism or to farm in the hills; others are the children of the hardy Europeans who came out 50 years ago (see chapter 10).

6

Charles Darwin and Galapagos

The voyage of the *Beagle*

In September 1835 a small, three-masted brig, sailed into Galapagos waters. She was called HMS *Beagle*, and was captained by the aristocratic FitzRoy (a descendant of King Charles II), whose job was to chart lesser-known parts of the world.

It was FitzRoy's idea to have a naturalist on board to study the strange new animals and plants they were to find en route. This person would not be paid, so it had to be someone who was both deeply interested in the subject and

29   *Interior of the* Beagle.

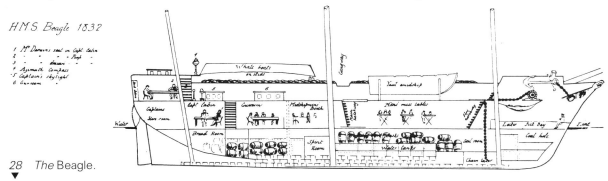

HMS Beagle 1832

1 Mr Darwins seat in Capt. Cabin
2 - " - Poop
3 - " - drawers -
4 Azimuth Compass
5 Captain's skylight
6 Gunroom

28   *The* Beagle.

who could afford to pay his way. That man was Charles Darwin.

It is surprising that Darwin, a man who was to change completely our ideas about the world, had shown little promise at school. His father once said, "You care for nothing but shooting, dogs and rat-catching, and you will be a disgrace to yourself and all your family!" By today's standards he would never have got into university. He did get a place at Edinburgh to study medicine, but was more interested in hobbies such as geology. He never finished his course, but, to please his father, studied Divinity at Cambridge with the idea of becoming a parson. Though academically he was of only middling ability, his enthusiasm for natural history was noted by his professors and he was recommended for the post on the *Beagle*.

When FitzRoy took Darwin on he was only 23, and it was to be five years before he would see home again. They were to sail around the world, giving him the chance to explore the rainforests of Brazil, the icy wastes of Patagonia and the high Andes of South America. The visit to Galapagos had been planned as a short stop on the return journey, by which time Darwin would have become an experienced observer. It was a stroke of luck that he had been picked for this unique cruise.

At that time people thought that the planet was only a few thousand years old, and that all species had been created at the same time, by God, as described in the Book of Genesis in the Bible. Darwin's observations were to make him realize that the Earth was millions of years older, and that over time some species had become extinct, whilst others had changed their shape or size. He experienced the effects of a bad earthquake in Chile, which made him realize that the planet, too, was in a state of change.

Darwin's first impressions of Galapagos

During the five weeks that the *Beagle* spent in Galapagos waters, FitzRoy was busy mapping the islands, whilst Darwin went ashore to

30   Charles Darwin in 1840.

collect plants, rocks, insects and birds. The unusual life-forms and their adaptations to the harsh place made a deep impression on him and eventually helped to inspire his revolutionary theory on the evolution of life.

The Galapagos provided a kind of model of the world in miniature. He realized that these recently pushed up volcanoes were young in comparison with the age of the Earth, and that the life in the islands showed special adaptations. Yet the plants and animals also showed similarities to those from the South American continent, where, he guessed, they had come from originally.

"The natural history of these islands is eminently curious, and well deserves

attention. Most of the organic productions are aboriginal creations, found nowhere else; there is even a difference between the inhabitants of the different islands; yet all show a marked relationship with those of America, though separated from that continent by an open space of ocean, between 500 and 600 miles in width. The archipelago is a little world within itself, or rather a satellite attached to America, whence it has derived a few strange colonists. Considering the small size of these islands, we feel more astonished at the number of their aboriginal beings, and at their confined range. Seeing every height crowned with its crater, and the boundaries of most of the lava-streams still distinct, we are led to believe that within a period, geologically recent, the unbroken ocean was here spread out. Hence both in space and time, we seem to be brought somewhat near to that great fact — that mystery of mysteries — the first appearance of new beings on this earth"
(Charles Darwin, *Voyage of HMS Beagle*, 1845).

Darwin realized that the life on the islands had probably come out by chance drifting, swimming or flying from the mainland (see chapter 9) and had not been created on the spot. Once the plants and animals had arrived, they evolved into forms better suited to the strange environment in which they found themselves.

Tameness

Darwin was an acute observer, and one of the first things that struck him was that all the animals on these isolated islands were extremely tame:

"A gun here is almost superfluous, for with the muzzle I pushed a hawk off the branch of a tree. One day, whilst lying down, a mocking-thrush alighted on the edge of a pitcher, made of the shell of a tortoise, and began to sip the water; it allowed me to lift it from the ground whilst seated on the vessel."

He attributed this tameness to the lack of predatory mammals.

Reptilian monsters or gentle giants?

The largest animals Darwin found were reptiles: the giant tortoises and the iguanas (large lizards) which were, despite their fierce appearance, plant-eaters. Darwin guessed that

31 Giant tortoises of the Galapagos. ▶

large tortoises could once be found all over the world, but had become extinct in most places because of competition from the more agile mammals. It is true that today they can be found only on remote islands where land mammals never arrived.

"As I was walking along I met two large tortoises, each of which must have weighed at least two hundred pounds: one was eating a piece of cactus, and as I approached, it stared at me and slowly stalked away; the other gave a deep hiss, and drew in its head. These huge reptiles seemed to my fancy like some antedeluvian [before the Flood] animals. The few dull-coloured birds cared no more for me, than they did for the great tortoises."

At the time of Darwin's visit the tortoises

32   Sailor with a boathook for turning over tortoises.

were still hunted and eaten. Darwin himself recommended roast tortoise: ". . . the flesh on it is very good; and the young tortoises make excellent soup."

One remark made by Mr Lawson, the English vice-governor of the colony, really made Darwin think: ". . . He could tell by looking at a tortoise which island it came from". Each island's tortoises had a distinctive shell type. Some were domed whilst others had high "saddle"-shaped necks. It began to dawn on Darwin that life on each island was unique, and that the Galapagos were a "laboratory of evolution", where new species were being modified from variations of others.

33a Four variations of beak size of the Galapagos finches.

33b An example of large-beaked finches.

Darwin's Finches

The "dull-coloured birds" turned out to be an interesting group of finches found only in Galapagos. When Darwin studied his collection, he found several species, each with a different beak size and shape depending on whether the bird ate nuts, seeds, grubs, or insects. We now know of 13 species, each with its own method of earning a living.

Biologists now call these "Darwin's Finches", and use them as an example of how the descendants of one ancestor can evolve into several species as they adapt to different conditions. There is even one kind that uses a cactus spine or twig as a tool to dig out grubs from bark. (See Fig. 34.)

Origins

What Darwin saw in Galapagos and on the voyage took years to develop in his mind. He built up evidence, like a lawyer on a big case, and twenty years later published the all-embracing theory in *The Origin of Species by means of Natural Selection* (1859). It was to cause quite a storm.

Natural selection

Darwin proposed that Natural Selection was the means by which populations, and eventually species, changed. In any group of a species there are different types of individuals, e.g. tortoises with long necks or with short necks. On some islands it would have been an advantage to have a longer neck, because in times of food shortage these tortoises would have done better, and produced more young. If the long neck were an inheritable characteristic, then eventually the tortoises on those islands would all tend to have longer necks. Elsewhere, where food was abundant and ground vegetation dense, short necks may have been naturally "selected" over time. Later scientists called this "Survival of the Fittest", which means that it is those who are best suited to the environment which survive and reproduce. It is a simple theory, but it took years to build up the evidence for it.

Why do you think it took Darwin so long to publish his theory? At that time people took the Bible literally. They believed that the world was created in seven days, and that today's species were all saved from the Great Flood by Noah. Darwin did not want to upset the religious and scientific community, and it was only when another scientist called Wallace arrived at a similar conclusion to his own, that he dared to publish a paper on evolution. A fierce debate raged over it. Ironically, his former Captain,

34 *Woodpecker finch using a twig as a tool to probe for grubs.*

FitzRoy, maintained that Darwin was a heretic and denounced him.

Darwin married on his return from the voyage, and spent the rest of his life quietly writing and researching in Kent. He is now recognized as the man who, ". . . provided a foundation for the entire structure of modern biology" (Julian Huxley).

7

Life on land

Every plant and animal is part of at least one "food chain". This represents successive stages in food (or energy) levels as one organism consumes another. All food chains begin with a *primary producer* which is a plant. Plants are the only organisms that can use energy from the sun and turn it into food. In doing so they also produce oxygen – and so they are very useful, since other living things are continually using up oxygen as well as food.

A food chain

Here is an example of a food chain found in Galapagos:

sun → grass → grasshopper → lizard → snake

The grasshopper is said to be the *primary consumer* as it feeds directly on the plant. The plant is turned into animal matter, the grasshopper, which in turn is consumed by the lizard (the next link in the chain). An animal which eats another animal is called a *carnivore* or *predator*. The final animal in the chain is called the top predator, in this example a snake. If a hawk were to eat the snake, where would it fit in the chain? Which would be the top predator? Try to work out a food chain found in your garden or local park, involving a common wild animal or insect.

Food webs

Nature is not as simple as the above example, however, as most animals provide food for more than one species. Several food chains are woven together into a network called a *food web*.

A creature that lives on another animal to obtain its food is called a *parasite*. Find one on the food web in Fig. 35. A successful parasite is one that does not kill its host.

The web is further complicated by those organisms that do not kill prey but scavenge on dead creatures, for example the Lava Gull (see p. 46). Micro-organisms that aid decay also have a valuable role in food webs. Where in this example would you place them?

The study of how organisms inter-relate is called "ecology". Islands make good places to

35 A food web. Can you put direction arrows on this to indicate possible orders of consumption?

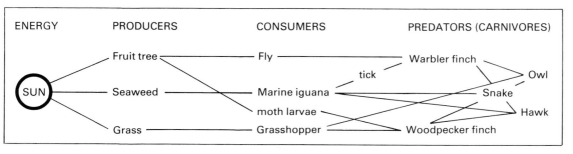

study ecology as their food chains are somewhat less complicated than those on continents.

Island peculiarities

Why do you think creatures found on isolated islands are often strikingly different from those found on continents?

In isolation, evolution proceeds along different lines. The lack of large mammalian predators in Galapagos has meant that most species there evolved without fear. We saw how Darwin remarked on this in chapter 6. Mockingbirds, for example, are so cocky that they will come and untie your shoelace or sit on your hat.

Another peculiarity of islands is that some animals evolve into larger sizes than their relatives elsewhere. The most striking example of this is the giant tortoise. Over one metre across, these lumbering giants have

36a "Dome" type Galapagos tortoise.

36b "Saddle-back" tortoise.

become the symbol of Galapagos. Darwin recognized how they differed from island to island, but that broadly speaking there are two main shapes: on islands where they have to reach up high to obtain fruits, they have longer necks and a "saddle-back" — for example, the race found on Española island; on islands with denser vegetation, where food is found lower but where tortoises have to push through thickets, they are "dome-shaped".

The Galapagos cormorant is also much larger than cormorants elsewhere, but it has an even more peculiar trait; it has completely lost the ability to fly. Can you think of any other wild birds that cannot fly? Under what circumstances would flying be unnecessary to a bird?

Cormorants here have evolved better swimming and diving ability at the expense of flying. Over the years their wing-size has been reduced, but their overall size has increased. They can now go deeper underwater than

37 A flightless cormorant shows the remains of its wings.

before, but are too heavy to fly.

On land, many birds, such as the mocking-bird, which is similar in size to the thrush, do not fly a great deal because of the abundance of food on the ground and the small number of predators. The Galapagos rail and dove hardly ever fly. If a population of humans were left isolated on the islands for millions of years, how do you think they would evolve over time?

Reptiles

The absence of large mammals has meant that the islands are dominated by reptiles on land. Darwin noted, "These islands appear paradises for the whole family of reptiles". Can you think why reptiles should be so successful?

Many visitors seeing these ugly reptiles mistakenly believed that they were a remnant of the age of dinosaurs. In fact, as we saw in chapter 3, the archipelago is quite young geologically (4 million years). The animals have evolved rapidly from mainland ancestors that somehow crossed the 1000-km stretch of ocean.

Reptiles have done well in Galapagos as they are tolerant to extremes of temperature and need little fresh water. They would also have been able to survive the journey out (see chapter 9).

Surprisingly, despite their fearsome appearance, the reptiles are mostly herbivores. Only the lava lizards, geckos and snakes are

38 Lava lizard.

carnivorous. The giant tortoises graze on grasses and cacti, and land iguanas are partial to prickly-pear fruits, though they first roll them with their feet to remove the spines! Marine iguanas are perhaps the most unusual diners, as they feed exclusively on seaweed.

All reptiles are "cold-blooded", that is, they regulate their temperature by behaviour, by getting in or out of the sun. They cannot lose heat by sweating or panting. The large size of a tortoise makes it a kind of "storage heater". During the day it slowly heats up; in the afternoon it will move to a shady spot. The heat is retained into the night, but the tortoise will gradually cool until dawn.

Land iguanas spend much of their time sunning themselves on the rocks. When they get too hot they hide in burrows underground. Marine iguanas cool down considerably when they are feeding at sea, and so their problem is how to warm up. They "sun-bathe" in herds on the black lava, their dark colour helping them to absorb more heat.

Marine iguanas impressed Darwin with their unique adaptations to a semi-marine life (flattened faces, rasping teeth and claws for clinging on to rocks in the surf). He did, however, remark that this kind of iguana was "a hideous-looking creature, of a dirty black

40 Marine iguana feeding on algae.

41 Giant prickly pear cactus tree. The fruit of these trees is relished by the tortoises.

39 Land iguana.

colour, stupid and sluggish in its movements".

Marine iguanas are found on the shores of nearly all the islands, but concentrate in groups where the best algae, called sea-lettuce, is to be found. Only the large adults go out to sea to feed; the young ones wait until their food is exposed at low tide. What dangers do you think there would be for small iguanas at sea?

At sea marine iguanas hold their breath, usually for about 15 minutes at a time, and go as deep as 12 m below the surface. How long can you manage to hold your breath under water? One of the sailors on the *Beagle* tried an experiment:

"A seaman on board sank one [an iguana] with a heavy weight attached to it, thinking thus to kill it; but when, an hour afterwards, he drew up the line, it was quite active."

The iguanas survive these dives by slowing down their hearts and altering their blood circulation – remarkable creatures indeed.

Island ecology

In chapter 2 we saw how the larger islands have vertical bands of climate that directly affect the plants that grow at different altitudes (Fig. 9). The bigger an island, the greater the variety of habitats, and so the larger the number of species we find. A habitat is a place with a particular kind of environment for the mixture of species (community) that lives there.

Here is a list of Galapagos habitats and organisms. Pair them correctly:

Habitat	Community of organisms
A. Sea-shore	1. grass, grasshoppers, ground finch, hawk
B. Lava-flow	2. trees, vegetarian finches, tortoises
C. Humid forest	3. cactus, lava lizard, dry-zone bushes
D. Upland moor	4. algae, marine iguana, crab, seabirds

Another factor that determines the number of species on a particular island is its distance from other islands and its distance from the mainland, in other words, how isolated it is. (In chapter 9 we shall see how organisms get out to islands in the first place.)

The more isolated islands, such as Española, Darwin and Genovesa, are also the ones with the smaller numbers of species. However, the species that do occur there seem to have evolved to become even more different from those of the same species on the central islands. For instance, on Española, the marine iguanas are much more colourful, the mocking-birds have longer beaks, and the lizards are much bigger than elsewhere.

The most striking case of evolution acting in isolation is on the remote island of Wolf. Here, the sharp-beaked ground finch has turned into a "vampire finch". The bird hops on to seabirds

Mutual relationships

In nature we can see many examples of relationships between particular animals and plants. An interesting case in Galapagos is that between tortoises and the prickly pear cactus. On the northern islands, where no tortoises have lived, the cactus forms low, spreading plants with soft spines.

On the tortoise islands the prickly pears have grown into giant tree-like forms with hard spines. In this way the trees defend themselves against being eaten by browsing tortoises. When the fruits are mature they drop off the plant, and the seeds produced germinate better for having passed through the gut of the reptiles who wait below. In this way the plants thrive and so do the tortoises.

Another example of a mutual relationship, in this case where two animals benefit from each other, is that between some small birds and land iguanas. The birds (ground finches and mockingbirds) remove ticks and other parasites from the iguanas' skins. So the iguanas get a cleaning whilst the birds get a meal. An iguana will actually stand up in a "cleaning position" when a bird hops on to it. A similar thing happens with tortoises, who stick out their necks when they want to be cleaned.

and, instead of removing ticks as elsewhere, it pecks a hole at the wing base of the bigger bird and feeds on blood!

Food niches

On the central islands, where there are several species of finch in the same community, the birds avoid competition with each other by each species having its own "food niche", or way of earning a living. Another way of describing the food niche is the role the species plays in the community. As we saw in chapter 6, some finches are "nut-crackers" with parrot-like beaks; others are seed-eaters, with smaller beaks; whilst the insectivorous or "wood-pecker" finches are further specialized, and even use a "tool".

Within the archipelago, competition occurs among the population of each species – which is how natural selection works (see chapter 6).

In the more crowded mainland habitats, competition is much fiercer, as other species try to take over the same niche. If one of the specialized Galapagos creatures were taken to the tropical forests of South America (where its ancestors had come from), do you think it would survive?

Endemism

An animal or plant is said to be "endemic" if it is naturally restricted to a particular area or region. In Galapagos the word is useful as some species are endemic to individual islands (e.g. the Española island lava lizard), while others are endemic to the whole archipelago (e.g. marine iguanas). A non-scientific equivalent would be "special". All the reptiles described in this chapter are endemic to the Galapagos archipelago. They are found nowhere else.

8

Life and the sea

Sitting for well over two hours, staring at the blue Pacific Ocean out of the window of the plane to Galapagos Islands, made me realize how far away from the nearest land they are. The Galapagos are true oceanic islands. All life there is connected in some way with the sea. In chapter 7 we looked at a typical web of life on an island; it included marine iguanas, which live on land but feed at sea. The food chains of land, coasts and deep sea are all intertwined into a complex web of life. Most activity is concentrated along the coast, where two environments meet and provide habitats for birds, reptiles, sea mammals, fish and a myriad of invertebrates such as the colourful "Sally-Lightfoot" crab.

In this chapter we shall examine parts of the oceanic web of life, and look in detail at some of the animals that have starring roles in it. In chapter 2 we saw how Galapagos is uniquely blessed with both cool and warm water environments. This explains why there is such a variety of creatures there.

42   Illustrated web of life for the Galapagos waters.

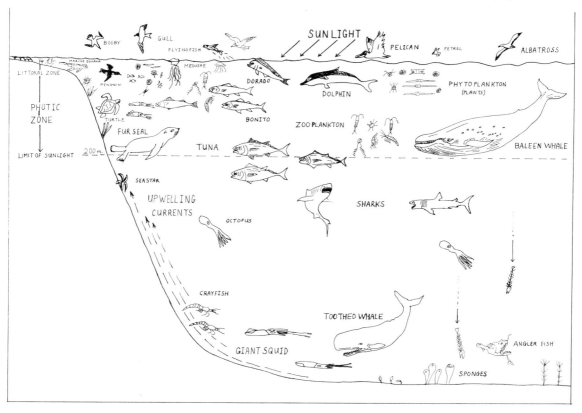

The oceanic web of life

Fig. 42 shows an illustrated web of life for Galapagos waters. Which is the zone where light penetrates and plants occur? Find a plankton-eating organism. Find a flesh-eater (carnivore or predator). Where do dead animals decompose because of bacteria?

The middles of oceans are not normally fertile places, which is why they are so clear and blue. All food chains begin with sunlight acting upon plant-life to photosynthesize oxygen and food out of minerals and carbon dioxide (CO_2). In an ocean food chain, the plant-life is *phytoplankton*. These are consumed by small fish and tiny drifting creatures called *zooplankton*, the herbivores in the chain. In turn, they are eaten by the predatory fish or birds. The whole process is dependent on light and nutrients getting to the plant life, and that is why the phytoplankton occur only in the top layers of the sea where light penetrates – the photic zone. Below a depth of 200 m there is very little life. Unfortunately, all the dead and decaying material falls to the deep, where the decaying material falls to the deep, where the nutrients remain until strong currents bring them up.

Now let us look in more detail at some of the important animals found in and around the waters of Galapagos.

Long-distance travellers

Islands make useful stop-over places for the world's most accomplished travellers, seabirds. Find out how migrating birds navigate for long distances at sea when they are out of sight of land.

Even the most jagged rock becomes a roosting spot for numbers of seabirds, whilst the flatter islands become breeding grounds and nurseries. The sky above these colonies is always filled with flocks of wheeling frigate-birds and boobies. On some islands there are so many that you have to step over them to be able to walk about. Their shrieking and squawking accompany you everywhere.

Many seabirds used the Galapagos as a stopping-off place on their migrations, and eventually several species made the islands their permanent home. The abundant fish and warm climate were too good to pass by. Out of 19 resident species, five are endemic to the archipelago. Some of them are associated with the cold Peru Current whilst others were brought by the warmer waters of the North Equatorial Current.

43 *Flow chart of one food web found in the sea off Galapagos. some of the arrows linking certain creatures have been purposely omitted. Where do you think these should go?*

44 *Seabirds of the Galapagos ▶*
a *Flightless cormorant**
b *Masked booby*
c *Red-footed booby*
d *Lava gulls**
e *Galapagos penguin**
f *Blue-footed booby*
g *Swallow-tailed gull**
h *Tropicbird*
i *Frigatebird*
j *Waved albatross**
k *Pelican*
*Species endemic to Galapagos

Since there is not room here to describe each species of bird in detail, some photographs of the most common ones are included. All these birds depend on the surrounding seas for their food. The boobies, a kind of gannet, are expert divers. When they find a shoal of fish or squid they plunge down into the water, diving several metres below the surface to seize their prey. Often they plunge in synchronized groups, which probably confuses the fish and makes it easier to catch them. The frigates, huge black birds with a forked tail and a wing span of two metres, have a different fishing technique. They fly along just above the water's surface and pluck out fish with their long hooked bills. Alternatively, they fly around, waiting for returning boobies or gulls; then they attack one of these until it spits out its meal and, with a graceful swoop, one of the frigates can promptly steal the food for itself.

How seabirds avoid competition

Most seabirds eat varieties of fish or crustaceans. To ensure that they do not waste time fighting over the same food, nature has arranged that each species feeds in its own way, time and place.

Look at the three kinds of booby. They all feed off similar fish, so how do they avoid competing for these? The Masked booby and Swallow-tailed gull both fish in the same waters, so how does the gull avoid fishing at the same time as the booby?

Courtship display

The Waved albatross of Galapagos spends much of the year in the air, travelling long distances around the Pacific, seldom settling on the water. It returns to one island, Española, to breed. These large yellow and white birds arrive in April after their "annual vacation". The younger ones arrive first and begin an elaborate courtship ritual or "dance" to establish a mate. Later on in May or June the older pairs arrive. They spend much less time courting and mate straight away. The display dance follows several steps in sequence, such as "sway-walking", "sky-pointing" and finally "bill-clacking", which is like a noisy duel with their long, heavy bills. Once the pairs have formed, the couple may stay together for several seasons. Do you think courtship display could play a part in the evolutionary process of "natural selection"?

Probably the most amusing sight in the Galapagos is the courtship dance of the Blue-footed booby. This is performed by young Bluefoots, who use the dance to check out likely partners to see who would make a suitable mate. First the male will "sky-point" at the female. If she responds with a similar posture, they will parade by each other, each in

Feeding methods of seabirds

Bird	Food	How caught	Where caught
Penguin	small fish	underwater swimming	cold inshore water
Cormorant	bottom-living fish, octopus	deep swimming	cold inshore water
Albatross	squid, large fish	sea surface	well offshore
Bluefoot booby	fish	plunge-diving	close inshore
Masked booby	fish	plunge-diving	between islands
Redfoot booby	fish	plunge-diving	outside islands
Swallow-tailed gull	squid and flying fish	surface-diving at night	between islands
Lava gull	scavenger		coast
Frigate-bird	fish	sea surface and steals from other birds	between and outside islands

turn waving its bright blue feet. They then offer each other bits of nesting material, which is somewhat odd as they never actually build a nest: the eggs are just laid on the ground. They take it in turns to incubate the eggs and feed the chicks.

Frigate-bird males put on a spectacular "show" when they are trying to attract a female. They inflate a huge red throat pouch, like a red balloon; there is much flapping of their extra-long wings and an unearthly "gobbling" sound is made.

On the beach

Of all the animals popular with visitors, the sea-lions and fur seals are top of the list. Both belong to the family of eared seals (*Otaridae*). These playful creatures resemble each other at first sight, but can be distinguished in several ways.

Comparion between sea-lions and fur seals

Sea-lion	Fur seal
lives on beaches	lives on rocky shores
feeds in daytime	feeds at night
longer neck and body	shorter and fatter
snout long and narrow	squat bear-like face
fur thin and light brown	fur thick and dark brown
moves easily on land	moves with difficulty on land
eyes small	eyes large

The sea-lions are cousins of the talented Californian sea-lion used by circuses to perform tricks. Most Galapagos beaches have numbers of sea-lions enjoying the good life of sunbathing, swimming and fishing. When

45a Galapagos sea-lion.

b Fur seal cub

breeding time comes, usually in the cool season, the large "beachmaster" males get aggressive in defending their so-called "harem" of about 20 females, and will chase away interlopers — including inquisitive humans! The young, however, will let you go close to them, and often come close for an inquiring sniff.

Fur seals are less friendly, probably as they were ruthlessly hunted, almost to extinction, during the eighteenth and nineteenth centuries. Numbers are now approaching 40,000 (almost as many as sea-lions). They prefer the steep, rocky shores, out of the sun. They come from a family of creatures that is normally found in the Antarctic. Look at the illustrated oceanic web of life (Fig 42). What creatures could be a danger to seals and sea-lions? Check with the flow chart (Fig 43).

During the warm season the tracks of marine turtles in the sand are a common sight on beaches. Females come ashore, usually at night, to lay their 80 or so ping-pong-ball-like eggs. These are laid in shallow holes dug in the sand. Unfortunately for the hatchlings that struggle out 55 days later, all kinds of predators are waiting to eat them when they emerge: frigates, herons, rats, crabs and beetles. One or two will "run the gauntlet" and survive to become adults, and will then return to the same beach years later, to leave *their* eggs. Turtles are an endangered species, and are protected internationally. Find out where else turtles are found. Why are they in danger?

Beneath the waves

Below the waves of Galapagos waters there is another world, just as fascinating as that on land. It is much less fully explored and can be observed only by those visitors who are equipped with masks and snorkels. Deeper exploration requires a Scuba diving tank. Find out who invented Scuba apparatus and how it works. Can you work out what SCUBA stands for?

Galapagos waters are chilly by tropical standards, so corals do not build up into great

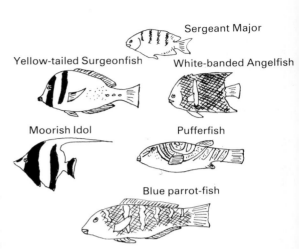

46   Some Galapagos inshore fish.

reefs, but small corals provide habitats for small reef fish. Find out why "puffer fish" or "blow-fish" are so called. Why do you think the "Sergeant Major" got its name?

Fish are important at different levels of the food web in Fig 42. They range from tiny plankton feeders to large carnivores like sharks. Some of the fish, such as *Bacalao*, or salt cod, and spiny lobsters, have a commercial value for local consumption and export. After tourism, fishing provides the second largest portion of the islanders' income. The recent creation of a marine reserve around the islands has meant that there is some conflict of interest between conservation and fishing.

Athletes and giants of the deep

Dolphins and whales can be seen frequently in Galapagos waters. They are warm-blooded mammals, like ourselves, and breathe air through a "blow-hole". To keep warm in the icy depths they have a thick fatty layer beneath the skin, called "blubber". It was for this blubber that they were once extensively hunted, as it contained an oil which had many uses.

The whale family, *cetaceans*, is divided into those which have teeth, and so are top predators of the ocean, and the plankton

feeders. It is ironic that the world's largest creatures, the filter-feeding whales, live off the smallest creatures, plankton. They do so with the aid of a whalebone or *baleen*. Why is it that creatures in the sea can grow to greater sizes than any animal on land? What is the biggest creature on Earth?

The toothed whales include killer whales and their smaller cousins, dolphins and porpoises. Dolphins are the most common cetaceans seen by visitors. The bottle-nosed dolphin

47   Black-tipped sharks. Sharks are the top predators in coastal waters, yet there has been no record of attacks on humans, probably because fish are so abundant around Galapagos.

frequently approaches boats to sport-ride the "bow wave", the water pushed in front of ships as they move. As they playfully rush along you can hear them communicating with each other in high-pitched squeaks. Often, you wonder who is looking at whom.

9

How did they get there?

When the first lavas pushed their way above the blue waters of the ocean, they did not support any life. Gradually, over hundreds of years, they cooled and life began to take advantage of the new environment. How could plants and animals have got to these islands? What would they have needed to survive there? Which life-form is at the start of all food chains? Bearing this in mind, which was probably the first to colonize the islands?

48 *Mangrove plants. The fruits float, and so this is one of the first trees to establish itself on island shores.*

Where could colonizing organisms have come from?

Crossing the ocean

Just as tadpoles do not appear in your pond spontaneously, life on the islands did not appear by magic. Life-forms had to journey across the 1000 km divide of water. (As we saw in chapter 3, the islands are tips of undersea volcanoes and were never linked to the mainland.) The ancestors of today's life-forms must have developed from the early voyagers.

Crossing the wide stretch of ocean presents many dangers and difficulties and this is why, compared to the South American mainland, the Galapagos have relatively few species of organism. Freshwater fish, amphibians (such as frogs), mayflies and caddis flies are not found on Galapagos — none of them could survive immersion in salt water sea-crossing. Apart from two species of bat, the only mammals on land are small rats. The ocean divide acts as a kind of sieve, only letting through certain kinds of species.

Arrival by sea

On the shores of Ecuador and Panama there are swamps where large rivers reach the sea through jungle regions. Look up these two countries in an atlas and find the two "Gulfs" where the swamps are. Huge rafts of vegetation often break off the banks during floods and drift out to sea. The strong ocean currents that we saw in chapter 2 (which ones in particular?) could easily carry these in the direction of Galapagos.

Most of these rafts break up, get water-logged and sink, but some reach the archipelago. Such rafts might carry organisms that could survive the journey and make a landing on an island. A single log could contain wood-boring insects, grubs, seeds or even the egg of a bird or reptile. Reptiles themselves are suited to this method of transport as they have a waterproof skin and can survive for some time without food or fresh water. It is estimated that it would take a log about two weeks to drift out to Galapagos from South America. It is quite possible that the green mainland iguana first arrived in the archipelago in this way.

Tortoises float if they fall in water, and so could have drifted out themselves or rafted part of the way and floated the rest. Their ancestors were probably small, the gigantic size only evolving later, in the islands. Coastal plants such as mangroves have fruits that float and are salt-tolerant, so they almost certainly drifted out on their own. Sea turtles, sea-lions, fur seals and penguins are all good swimmers and with the aid of the currents could have made their own way out. Which animal

49 *Humidity in the highlands enables lichens and mosses to grow on the tops of trees.*

probably swam the furthest to make Galapagos its home? The only bee in Galapagos is the Carpenter Bee, which is a wood-borer. How do you think it arrived?

Arrival by air

Scientists have found that samples of air taken at high altitudes contain a surprising selection of spores, seeds and even insects. Storm winds over land blow all these up into the atmosphere, where they can travel great distances. At sea, rains are more likely to fall over islands because as air rises over them the water vapour held in it condenses. This rain would bring down seeds and spores.

Plants such as lichens, ferns and fungi have tiny spores which have been distributed throughout the world. In Galapagos these are found in the higher islands where the climate is moist enough to support them.

Flowering plants have heavier seeds, and so are less able to use this method. Some, however, like the dandelion family, have parachute-like mechanisms which aid wind dispersal. Not surprisingly, many members of this "weed" family are found on the islands, including one called *Scalesia* which has evolved into tree-like forms. Which other plant has evolved into tree-like forms? (See chapter 7.)

Bats, butterflies and land birds can fly, but

the Galapagos are not on a migration path between the Americas, so it is more likely that these creatures were initially blown off course by strong winds. Again, once they had arrived it made more sense to stay rather than risk the dangerous journey back. It is thought that the ancestor of all the finches was diverted accidentally in this way from Panama. Seabirds, on the other hand, are great fliers and their arrival poses no mystery.

Arrival of birds

Birds themselves often carry seeds, fruits and parasites. I have often seen seabirds landing with sticky seeds attached to their feathers. Eventually these get wiped off, a long way from where they were picked up. It has been estimated that 60 per cent of the plants in Galapagos arrived in this way. As you walk around the more densely vegetated parts of Galapagos you find many sticky or barbed seeds attached to your socks or trousers. Visitors are warned to be careful not to transport plants from one island to another, as they could upset the ecology by this inadvertent "hitch-hiking".

Birds also eat fruits and seeds which slowly digest in their gut and get deposited elsewhere. You may think that this would destroy the seed, but it has been shown that many seeds actually grow better after this treatment: for example, the Galapagos wild tomato germinates better after passing

through the gut of a mockingbird. Darwin was a great experimenter, and spent much time successfully germinating seeds that he picked out of bird excrement! Birds of prey, like hawks, which eat finches that have eaten seeds can transport the seed further from island to island.

Establishment of a colony

Arriving in the archipelago and surviving the danger of landing is not enough; to succeed and reproduce you need to find your environmental requirements. A tortoise, for example, would need fresh water, food in the form of suitable nutritious plants already flourishing, and shade from the adverse effects of the tropical sun. To continue the species it would also need a healthy mate of approximately the same age, and the right kind of soil in which to lay eggs. All these special needs further reduce the chance of successful colonization. Only a limited number of organisms could make the journey to the islands, and the number of these that survive is reduced to those which can find their habitat needs. Yet, given enough time, the necessary conditions do develop and, as time goes on, a larger number of habitats becomes available.

We can make a guess as to the sequence of colonization:
1. Lower plants, e.g. lichens.
2. Higher plants (wind pollinated), e.g. weeds.
3. Higher plants and their insect or bird

How did they get there?

Try to match up the species with their most likely method of transport:

A.	Galapagos tomato	1. Swam up from Antarctic aided by currents
B.	Giant tortoise	2. Flew down from the Caribbean
C.	Galapagos cotton	3. Floated out from Ecuador's coast
D.	Flamingo	4. Seed eaten by bird
E.	Sea-lion	5. Pregnant female rafted out from Panama
F.	Penguin	6. Seeds attached to bird's feathers
G.	Land iguana	7. Swam down from California

pollinators, e.g. *Palo Santo* trees and tree finches.
4. Herbivores, e.g. tortoises.
5. Carnivores, e.g. hawks.

Compare this sequence to the food chain on page 37. Are there any similarities? Why should this be so?

We have seen that all food chains begin with plants, so vegetation would have had to arrive and be established before animals could survive. Until the lava had cooled and weathered to produce soil that stores water, plants would have come to nothing. Some recent lava flows are still devoid of life.

Pioneer plants

The first colonizers are the hardy plants that need little soil or moisture. On lava these are the tubular cactus, *Brachycereus* (Fig. 51) and the tiny herb *Mollugo*. On the more dusty ash the first plant to appear is a shrub called *Tiquilia*. These are called "pioneer plants". Can you think of some pioneer plants that would colonize a newly-cleared wasteland site in your local area? How would they have arrived there?

On the arid lowlands, other plants that thrive in dry conditions appear. Some resist the drought by remaining dormant until the rains arrive, e.g. the *Palo Santo* tree; others develop spines and waxy leaves and remain green all year. An alternative strategy is that of succulent plants, such as the cactus, which store water from the wet season to use in the dry one.

Once the first rung in the ladder of the food chain has been established, the herbivores, and later the carnivores, are able to make successful landings.

Reproduction

Self-pollinating plants are those most likely to reproduce in an environment where there are only a few members of each species. Wind-

50 *The surface of Bartolomé island, showing the barrenness of small cinder or "spatter" cones.*

51a Brachycereus cactus grows straight out of arid lava.

51b "Palo Santo" trees. The Spanish name refers to the incense-like smell the wood gives off when it is burnt. The trees look dead, but are dormant until the rains come.

pollinated plants also have a better chance of reproducing than those that need special insects to pollinate them. For animals, too, the timing of arrival was crucial to their success. Most of them would have needed a pair to arrive together (unless the one that arrived was a pregnant female).

Once they had arrived and established a colony, the animals had the advantage of lack of competition from other species. With the islands to themselves they could, over generations, evolve into the new and peculiar forms found nowhere else.

Following man's comparatively recent arrival in the archipelago, he too has become an important introducer of species. Some botanists think humans have brought in, either by accident or intentionally, more species of plant than the birds have in the last few years. They estimate these to be almost 200 species of weeds and cultivated plants. What effect do you think this has on the native plants?

Man has also brought in domesticated animals such as cattle and pigs, which have then become feral, and, by accident, such pests as rats and fire ants. Would you say most of the plants and animals arrived by chance, or did they set out with the intention of colonizing

51c Tiquila shrubs are pioneer plants on ash slopes.

the islands? There are many families of plants and animals which do not appear in Galapagos. Why do think this is so? Would you consider the introduction of organisms by man a natural or unnatural colonizing process?

10

Man and the Galapagos today

In 1984 most of the world learnt of Galapagos for the first time. A fire broke out on Isabela and spread around the slopes of Sierra Negra volcano. Soon the world's press became concerned with the fate of the tortoises that lived there – as it could have been the end of that "race" of tortoise. The National Park Service moved a group of 20 tortoises to safety and, with the aid of the Ecuadorian army, built a 50 km–long fire-break that eventually contained the blaze. The fire continued smouldering underground and it was not until five months after it began that it was completely burnt out. The fire was an accidental result of crop-burning by settlers, and is an example of how dangerous man can be in a fragile environment.

Man the destructive species

We have already seen historical examples of how man has upset the islands' ecosystem. The buccaneers killed tortoises and left behind black rats, which crawled ashore when the sailors hauled their ships out to careen them. The rats wiped out the endemic rodents and attacked tortoise eggs.

British and American whalers took hundreds of thousands of tortoises for food and oil, reducing several sub-species to virtual extinction. Hunters nearly exterminated fur seals in Galapagos by the 1930s; Captain Morrell boasted of taking 5,000 seals in two months.

Settlers cleared land and forest for cultivation and pasture and brought with them goats, donkeys and cattle which rapidly stripped the vegetation on which the reptiles depended. Allowing goats ashore was probably even more destructive than hunting had been. Similarly, introduced cats, dogs and pigs turned feral, all causing havoc with the native fauna, especially ground-nesting birds such as the dark-rumped petrel. They could still threaten the penguins and cormorants today.

Island ecosystems are extremely vulnerable to organisms introduced from other areas. The native creatures are so specialized to the simplified environment that they cannot compete with the intruders.

Even scientists contributed to the decimation, with their passion for "collecting" during the early twentieth century; they removed some of the last remaining tortoises from islands where they later became extinct. How do you think the attitude of scientists towards collecting animals has changed over the last 50 years?

The adverse effect of man has been recognized and attempts are now being made to reverse the situation.

Galapagos National Park

The first laws protecting the fauna in the archipelago were passed by the Ecuadorian Government in 1934; but nothing practical was done until 1959, when the Galapagos National Park was set up. This included all the islands except those parts already colonized by people. The park covers about 97 per cent of the archipelago. In 1968, when tourism was just beginning, the Galapagos National Park Service (GNPS) was appointed to control the whole

52 A hawk resting on one of the National Park monuments. The writing warns visitors that the wildlife is protected by law.

53 Sign of the Galapagos Natonal Park central office.

park. It may be said that a conflict of interests arose between the island settlers and the park authorities. What do you think these could be?

Objectives of the Galapagos National Park
1. *Conservation* – preservation of scenery
   – protection of native species
   – eradication of introduced animals and plants
   – control of human activity
2. *Visitor use* – tourism
3. *Education* – of visitors and residents to an awareness of conservation, and to provide information
4. *Scientific research*

Do you think all these aims have equal priority? If not, which one is the most important? Rank them in the order of priority you would give them.

The first task was to survey the islands and to find out the size of populations of all the species. This was done in tandem with an international group of scientists, named the Charles Darwin Foundation. It was in 1959, one hundred years after the publication of Darwin's *Origin of Species*, that the Charles Darwin Foundation was set up with the aid of UNESCO (the United Nations Educational, Scientific and Cultural Organization). It is an independent organization and is now funded by various bodies such as the World Wildlife Fund.

A research station

The first priority of the Charles Darwin Foundation (CDF) was to build a research station for visiting scientists. Work began immediately at Academy Bay on Santa Cruz island, near the village of Port Ayora, and the station was opened in 1964. From then on the repair of the archipelago's damaged ecology began in earnest. The station was named the Charles Darwin Research Station (CDRS).

Surveys by the scientists and park personnel revealed where tortoises and iguanas were most endangered. Two programmes were started. The first was to eradicate introduced species. Goats, being the biggest problem, were eliminated on the islands of Santa Fe, Rabida, Española, Marchena, Pinta and the islet of Plazas. But on large islands like Santiago, where there are over 100,000 goats, control still remains a daunting task for a handful of men equipped with old shotguns.

The second programme was to try to breed in captivity (in the CDRS) the most endangered species of tortoise and land iguana. For example, in the early 1960s on Española island there were only two male and eleven female tortoises. They were successfully bred and in 1975 the first tortoise young were returned to the wild. By 1985, 151 had been returned to Española. They seem to be doing well. The CDRS is breeding tortoises from five other islands, and land iguanas from Santa Cruz and Isabela.

Scientists come from all over the world to do research in Galapagos, using the CDRS as a base. If you travel around the islands, you may come across a strange bearded creature

lurking in the bushes with a notebook and a pair of binoculars!

Another role played by the CDRS is to help the Park Service to train the guides who work on the tour boats. It is the naturalist guides who educate the tourists and teach them about conservation, and at the same time prevent tourists from upsetting the animals.

Each year the number of visitors increases. There are now about 25,000 tourists a year. There are flights daily, except on Sundays, to

54   The tortoise-raising centre at Charles Darwin ▶
Research Station.

55   Tourist with a marine iguana, showing how tame the animals are.
▼

Baltra island, and a new service has started to San Cristóbal.

56 *Yacht which transports tourists around the islands.*

Galapageños

The people who live in the islands number about 6000, and call themselves Galapageños. They are a mixed group; some are descendants of European colonists of the 1930s, but most are people from the mountains and coasts of Ecuador who came to seek a new life on the islands. Most arrived in the last 20 years, to profit from the new industry of tourism.

The main settlements are on Santa Cruz, San Cristobal and Isabela, with a few people on Floreana and a military base on Baltra. By farming the highlands they produce bananas, avocados, sugar and yucca, but the only products exported are coffee and cattle.

Fishing for sea bass and grouper and diving for lobsters also brings in some income to the islands. Conservationists have raised concern about the need to protect the marine environment – as the underwater life is as unique as that on land. A "Marine Reserve"

A tourist's day

"At breakfast time, 7 a.m., our yacht has arrived at a new island. We have been travelling most of the night in the hands of our experienced crew. The cook serves a hearty breakfast of eggs, coffee and bread, and fresh pineapple and papaya add a tropical flavour.

Clutching our cameras in a plastic bag to avoid sea-spray, we race the breakers ashore in a *panga*, a flat-bottomed dinghy. Sea-lions greet us on the beach and the young pups approach us playfully. Pelicans dive-bomb into the surf. Bright red crabs disappear into crevices.

We walk at an easy pace for a couple of hours as the heat of the day builds up.

Cheeky mockingbirds peck at our feet, whilst hawks silently hover over us. Back on the beach we are ready for a dip in the blue, clear water.

Lunch on board is followed by a *siesta*. We motor-sail to another inlet, passing the historic Buccaneers' Cove on the way.

The afternoon visit is just as fascinating. We see contorted lava formations that look like the surface of Mars. The guide makes us stay on a special trail, marked by wooden stakes. Time for a snorkel back to the yacht, keeping an eye out for bull sea-lions, and marvelling at the colourful fish en route.

The long, warm evening is spent discussing the wonderful day, comparing notes with other passengers, and enjoying the star-filled sky."

was decreed in 1986, with a 3 km offshore limit.

In the long run it is the wildlife that attracts the tourists, and they bring in the most money to the national economy. So the locals benefit if the whole environment is protected. Tourism is the main hope for the future provided it remains strictly controlled. People are the latest and most potentially threatening Galapagos species.

The future

Of all the wild areas of the world, Galapagos has one of the best arguments in support of protection and conservation. The many unique organisms are endangered in many ways. Their isolation has made the islands into that "showcase of evolution" which inspired Darwin 150 years ago.

We have seen how fragile this isolated environment is and how steps had to be taken to try to restore the balance of nature. In 1979 the Galapagos islands were given "World Heritage Status" by UNESCO, and this has spurred international help and encouraged the Ecuadorian Government to back conservation measures.

Some suggest that tourists should be banned from the islands completely. This seems unreasonable, as carefully controlled tourism benefits the local economy and helps pay for conservation. Visitors have to obey park rules and are "policed" by the trained guides,

57   Groupers are the main fish caught in Galapagos.

who explain about the natural history in several languages. Recent studies show that the impact of visitors on wildlife has been minimal, although erosion of the trails is a problem. The GNPS is looking at ways of avoiding this, by changing the tourist trails or periodically re-routing them.

As more people become city-bound and urbanized, the importance of preserving wilderness areas increases. More National

58   The naval base on Santa Cruz island.

GALAPAGOS
NATIONAL PARK

E C U A D O R

RULES FOR
PRESERVATION

59 *Extract from the rules for the preservation of the Galapagos National Park.*

RULES FOR THE GALAPAGOS

NATIONAL PARK

Galapagos is yours to enjoy. Will your grandchild still have the chance to see it as you do?.-.Your ? is needed to protect it!

Don't leave anything more than footprints, don't t anything but exposed film. Please follow and ? enforce the following rules:

1 NO PLANT, ROCK OR ANIMAL SHOULD DISTURBED OR REMOVED. It is illegal : can do serious harm to the Island's ecologial (ditions.

2 BE CAREFUL NOT TO TRANSPORT ANY VE MATERIAL TO THE ISLANDS OR FR ISLAND TO ISLAND. Check your clothing b re landing on any of the islands for seeds or sects and destroy them or keep them on your ssel for disposal later. Do not bring them on Islands. Inadvertant transport of these mater represents a special danger. Each Island has unique fauna and flora and introduced plants animals can quickly destroy this uniqueness.

3 ANIMALS MAY NOT BE TOUCHED OR H/ DLED, All wild animals dislike this and ? quickly lose their remarkable tameness if t treated by human invaders.

4 ANIMALS MAY NOT BE FED. Not only ca? be dangerous to your own person but on a l term it can destroy the animals social struct? as in the land iguanas on South Plaza Islan?

5 DO NOT STARTLE OR CHASE ANY A MAL FROM IT'S RESTING OR NESTI SPOT.— Exercise extreme care among the b? ding colonies of sea-birds. Specially do not d? boobies, cormorants, gulls, or frigate birds f? their nests. Frigate bird nests on North Seym? should not be approached closer than 40 (130 ft.) while frigate bird and booby nests Tower island should not be approached closer t? 6 m. (20 ft.). These bird will fly from their n?

parks like Galapagos need to be set up to provide sanctuary for native species, and protect areas of outstanding natural interest which visitors can appreciate. These oceanic islands, in particular, are very special.

Glossary

archipelago   a group of geographically-related islands.
basalt   a dense, dark volcanic rock commonly found at oceanic volcanoes. Composed of material originating in the Earth's mantle.
buccaneer   a pirate of the seventeenth and eighteenth centuries who would, with the unofficial approval of the English crown, attack Spanish possessions in the Americas.
caldera   a large, collapsed volcanic crater.
careen   to take a wooden ship out of the water in order to repair the hull.
cinder   a common name for *scoria*, which is a highly gassy, viscous lava that forms small volcanoes or spatter-cones.
crust   the solid outer layer of the Earth that is divided into a thinner, denser oceanic crust and a thicker, lighter continental crust.
display   a particular behavioural pattern of one animal to another, as in courtship.
ecosystem   a community of organisms, interacting with one another, together with the environment in which they live.
endemic   native or special to a particular region; in Galapagos some species are endemic to one island, whilst others are endemic to the archipelago as a whole.
feral   word used to describe a domesticated animal that has reverted to the wild.
food chain   a link between plants, herbivores and carnivores that represents successive energy levels.
food web   the inter-relation of several food chains.
garua   a misty rain or drizzle typical of the cool season in Galapagos.
gyre   large-scale circular movement of an ocean current.
habitat   the place or environment where a plant or animal naturally lives or grows.
hotspot   a small volcanic centre in the ocean crust, away from the edge of a crustal plate, where magma rises from the upper mantle.
inversion   warm air overlying cool air.
invertebrates   animals without backbones; usually small, soft creatures that have hard outside shells.
lava   melted rock that reaches the surface and flows out of a volcano.
lichen   a primitive plant that is part algae and part fungus and often forms a crusty growth on rocks or dead trees.
magma   molten rock that comes up from the Earth's upper mantle.
mantle   the zone of the Earth's interior between the core and the crust. The upper mantle contains a partly melted zone on which the crustal plates move.
photic zone   the part of the ocean to which sunlight penetrates.
photosynthesis   the building up of nutrients by green plants using water, carbon dioxide and energy from the sun.
plate tectonics   a development of the theory of continental drift: that is, that the Earth's crust is split into irregular plates that move, and on which the continents ride. The theory explains why volcanoes and earthquakes occur where they do, at the plate boundaries.
predator   an animal that feeds on another by hunting.
rain-shadow   an area of land that gets little rain because it is on the leeward side of a mountain.
species   the fundamental unit of biological classification. The members of a species are generally very much alike and can all interbreed to produce fertile offspring.
spore   a non-sexual reproductive organ of non-flowering plants, such as fungi, mosses or ferns.
tuff   a layered rock, formed by fine volcanic particles or ash, that results from an explosive eruption.
viscosity   a measurement of the "stickiness" of a fluid, i.e. its resistance to flow.

Further reading

Brower and Porter, *The Flow of Wildness* (The Sierra Club, 1968)

Calder, Nigel, *The Restless Earth* (Penguin, 1978)

Darwin, Charles, *Journal of the Voyage of HMS Beagle* (John Murray, 1845)

Darwin Charles, *The Origin of Species* (John Murray, 1859)

Epler, White and Gilbert, *Galapagos Guide* (Libri Mundi, 1972)

Hickman, John, *The Enchanted Islands, The Galapagos Discovered* (A. Nelson, 1985)

Harris, Michael, *Birds of Galapagos* (Collins, 1974)

Jackson, Michael, *Galapagos: A Natural History Guide* (University of Calgary, 1985)

Lewin, R. and Thompson, S. *Darwin's Forgotten World* (Bison, 1978)

Melville, Herman, *The Encantades* (San Francisco, 1940)

Moorhead, Alan, *Darwin and the Beagle* (Penguin, 1971)

Perry, Roger, *The Galapagos Islands* (Dodd, Mead 1972)

Perry, Roger (ed.), *Galapagos – Key Environments* (Pergamon, 1984)

Thornton, Ian, *Darwin's Islands* (New York Natural History Press, 1971)

Treherne, John, *The Galapagos Affair* (Johnathan Cape, 1983)

Wittmer, Margret, *Floreana* (Michael Joseph, 1961)

Island Information

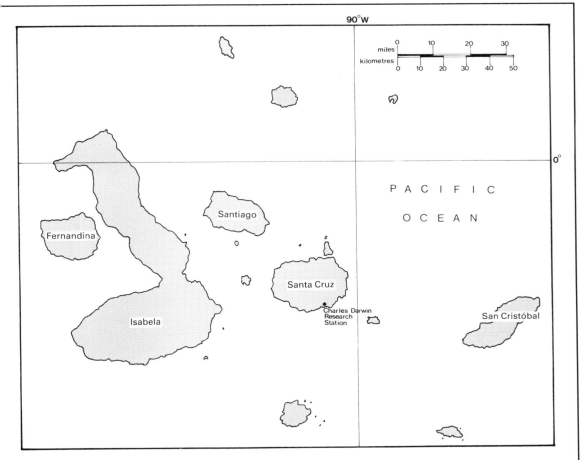

90°W

miles

kilometres

PACIFIC

OCEAN

Fernandina

Santiago

Santa Cruz

Charles Darwin
Research
Station

Isabela

San Cristóbal

0°

Government: The archipelago is a separate province of the Republic of Ecuador; it has a local Governor as head.

Total land area: 7,882 sq. km.

Largest island: Isabela, 4,588 sq. km.

Official title: Archipiélago de Colón.

Official language: Spanish.

Capital: Puerto Baquerizo Moreno (San Cristóbal island).

Inhabited islands: San Cristóbal, Santa Cruz, Floreana, Isabela, Baltra.

Total population: 6,000 (1982), now probably nearer 8,000.

Biggest town: Port Ayora, Santa Cruz, approximately 4,000 people.

Visitors: Approximately 25,000 per year.

Currency: The Sucre, same as mainland Ecuador, but US dollars accepted.

Defence: Naval base at each port, airforce base on Baltra.

Economy: Tourism and fishing.

Other Functions: Scientific research.

History of National Park:
1934 First protective laws passed in Ecuador.
1959 All islands declared National Park (except the colonized areas).
1959 Charles Darwin Foundation created with headquarters in Brussels, Belgium.

1964 Charles Darwin Research Station (CDRS) inaugurated.
1968 National Park Service began working under auspices of Ministry of Agriculture.
1969 Organized tourism began.
1986 Marine area declared National Reserve.

Index